ALBERT E. HUGHES, B.A.

What Your Handwriting Reveals

W Published by
Melvin Powers
ILSHIRE BOOK COMPANY
12015 Sherman Road
No. Hollywood, California 91605
Telephone: (213) 875-1711

First published in Great Britain by
Neville Spearman Limited
112 Whitfield Street, London W1P 6DP

Printed by

HAL LEIGHTON PRINTING COMPANY
P.O. Box 3952
North Hollywood, California 91605
Telephone: (213) 983-1105

Printed in the United States of America
ISBN 0-87980-365-7

CONTENTS

There is a principle which is a bar against all information, which is proof against all argument and which cannot fail to keep a man in everlasting ignorance. That principle is condemnation before investigation.

HERBERT SPENCER

To the memory of
Dr.med. and Dr.phil. George Strelisker
(1894-1962)
who taught me most of what I know
concerning graphology, characterology and depth-psychology

Not to discriminate every moment some passionate attitude in those around us is, on this short day of frost and sun, to sleep before evening.

WALTER PATER

PREFACE

This is both a practical and an academic book on graphology. From the practical point of view, I hope that it will be of considerable use to all who are engaged in character and personality assessments: banking and insurance officials, management consultants, sales managers, security officials, police officers, probation officers, social workers, clergymen, teachers, lawyers, doctors, etc.

From the academic point of view, I have discussed the scientific basis of graphology; the nature of character and personality; the comparison of handwriting-analysis with character and personality tests; the philosophical basis of graphology; the historical and developmental background of graphology; the much-disputed form-level concept of Ludwig Klages; the depth psychologies of Freud, Jung and Szondi; the inter-relationship between graphological and depth-psychological findings. Moreover, I have listed one hundred and fifty graphological works for the reader who wishes to pursue the matter further.

A.E.H.

4, Mountway Road,
Bishops Hull,
Taunton,
Somerset.

1 Graphology: The Science of Handwriting Analysis

There are two kinds of science, 'Naturwissenschaft' or natural science and 'Geisteswissenchaft' or mental/moral/spiritual science. This distinction has long been recognised in German-speaking countries but it is ignored or denied outside of the German cultural orbit.

Natural science is concerned with the repetitive phenomena of nature. In such a study, a finite number of variables is subjected to a quantifiable analysis. For example, in physics one can predict with absolute certainty the reactions of water to cooling between normal temperature and four degrees Centigrade and again between four degrees Centigrade and zero, subject to constant conditions of pressure. In psychology and character-ology, predictions with such a high degree of accuracy are impossible—a good graphologist can predict within an accuracy range of 87·88% and 95%. And a highly skilled graphologist can achieve a still higher percentage of accuracy.

But 'mind' is not nature and so the study of mind cannot be undertaken by the methodology of natural science. Indeed, the German word 'Geist' cannot be translated adequately into English—it means 'mind', 'spirit', 'culture', 'civilisation', etc. all rolled into one. History is the best example of the mental/moral/spiritual sciences. Unlike physics, which is concerned with the study of the repetitive phenomena of nature (the study of parts), history is concerned with study of a once-and-for-all phenomenon of Geist (the study of the whole). For instance, the signing of Magna Carta was a once-and-for-all phenomenon of Geist. Other examples are the unique configuration of my finger prints (from the science of cheirology), again *the unique configuration of my signature* when I signed a cheque at 2.30 p.m. yesterday, etc.

Thus do I claim that graphology is a Geisteswissenschaft and, as such, cannot be adequately studied within the terms of reference of natural science.

Natural science is a study of parts but the study of Geist is a study of the whole. Here it must be emphasised that a whole is not an *aggregate*—a mere summation of parts. It is *totality* which is more than the sum of the parts. From this it follows that any experimental or statistical investigations of Geist are something like intellectual original sin—they betray a fundamental misunderstanding of the subject. And any so-called psychology which insists on applying *only* the techniques of natural science must, by definition, be confined to the peripheral phenomena of neuro-physiology and anatomy.

The gift for studying 'mind', 'spirit', 'soul', etc. rests essentially upon a capacity for seeing meaning, structure and configuration within the world of phenomena, this means the ability to apprehend things symbolically. *Thus we have to have the whole before we can undertake to study the parts.* As Klages said, it is possible to analyse the whole into the parts but to compose the whole out of the parts is impossible *unless the idea which is to guide in the process of composition has already been extracted from the whole.*

Here I had better make another point clear. I am not opposed to the efforts of those excellent psychological and graphological experimenters who devote thousands of hours to the study of such physical details as muscular pressure, viscosity of ink, surface of paper, etc., etc. These studies make very valuable contributions to a natural science approach to the psychology of handwriting but it is a fundamental fallacy to assume that they can ever solve the problems of graphology—their methods preclude them from so doing.

The act of writing is a symbolical expression of Geist, of a whole. Now, either the laws relating to such expression are valid or they are not. If they are invalid then the theory and practice of graphology is bunk. And if they are valid then no amount of fragmentary and partial research can contribute significantly to —or detract significantly from—the study of handwriting as an expressive gesture of a whole. For instance, when the writing instrument moves into the upper zone of writing, it is so moved by the muscular activity of the extensors. When the instrument moves in the lower zone of the writing it is so moved by the flexors. But a preference for the upper zone symbolises adjustment by idealistic and non-instinctual behaviour, a preference for the lower zone symbolises adjustment by materialistic and instinctual (non-idealistic) behaviour. Of course, it is agreed that there could be no upper zone or lower zone writing without the co-ordination of flexor or extensor muscular activities, themselves activated by neuro-endocrine activities. But such neurophysiological and muscular activities are merely the somatic and natural expressions of the psyche which is Geist. To deny this is to play HAMLET without the Prince. Nor can this be explained by the theory of psycho-physical parallelism because it is not a case of a parallelism of independent phenomena.

When, therefore, a critic objects that somebody writes in a particular manner because he was taught that style by a teacher, I maintain that such an objection is invalid. The writer *retains* that style for individual and personal reasons of his own—he may well have introjected the imago of his favourite teacher. Again, when a critic points out that he is always changing his style of writing, I counter the objection by answering that this does not invalidate graphological theory and practice, it merely shows that the critic has a schizoid and/or hysteroid background. If a critic asks me what do I learn from the scribblings of a pre-school age child, I say that such scribbles are most revealing since such a child's expressions have not yet had to be confined to an individual arrangement of the conventionally accepted twenty-six letters of the alphabet.

It is always the proportion of tension between two opposites which reflects the particular activity of an individual mind. It is the minute oscillation between left and right, upward and downward movement, between tension and relaxation and all the other innumerable *polarities* which has to be observed and interpreted. For all our contradicting tendencies and directions in life are duly reflected and expressed in our handwriting. We are good and bad, egotistic and altruistic, selfish and interested in other people, optimistic or pessimistic, decided or undecided, confident or afraid, secure or frightened in any given time, place or circumstances. And we are never the same, oscillating from day to day, from hour to hour, sometimes from minute to minute, as we are always, so to speak 'tottering through life' with fluctuating thoughts and emotions, bound to convention, craving for freedom, hoping and despairing, thus our handwriting is undergoing a continuing change.

But all our experiences in life do not alter the fundamental structure of our character and temperament, though they can give us some new direction and stimulate a development within our inherited possibilities. *Thus all sudden changes in our handwriting do not transform its fundamental structure.* Changes occur and because changes occur our handwriting is variable. Although the expert graphologist is able to check different stages of child development and adolescence, to trace the progress of a patient undergoing psychotherapy, or to observe the effects of a new profession or of an unhappy marriage, it has to be admitted that our handwriting does not always register immediately all changes in our attitudes to life. This may be due to the fact that certain changes develop slowly, that we still cling to habitual movements and try to disguise (consciously or unconsciously) the change of our outlook or attitude. Many factors play a role in the performance of a handwriting and not all these factors can be taken into consideration in any single sample of script.

But the usual objections have no value. It does not matter, for example, whether or not a person disguises his handwriting (consciously or unconsciously). By experiment it has been discovered which features can be changed easily and which with difficulty. Arbitrary efforts of transformation in a handwriting may deceive a layman but they will not deceive an expert who knows all the funny tricks concerning the conscious and unconscious disguising of handwriting.

We all differ in our capacity to express our thoughts and feelings. Constitution, temperament or the whole endocrine make-up and, of course, our upbringing, stipulate the modes of our expression. Accordingly, some handwritings are far more expressive than others. But strangely enough, the extravagance

16

or poverty of expression is not always in agreement with the actual behaviour-pattern of the individual, as observed in the reactions of his daily life. Expressions of the face and gestures can easily be controlled and trained but *the handwriting unresistingly reveals all combinations and contradictions of our mental activities.* But it must be emphasised that there is no one characteral trait which is revealed by a single characteristic of handwriting. On the contrary, *a rigid evaluation of certain signs must lead to fallacies.* This shows the danger and the futility of consulting those graphological texts based on fixed signs. We cannot judge an isolated feature and apply it generally to the personality as a whole. It is not possible to solve the internal contradictions of the human organism and the polarity of such a complex unity as body-mind on such a simple basis. *Only the combination and inter-connection of all the characteristics of a handwriting will integrate into the uniqueness of the individual.* And as this uniqueness is conditioned by innumerable factors, it must be obvious that all these counter-balancing forces and tendencies cannot find their expression in one or two isolated features. For example, among these counter-balancing forces and tendencies are the arrangement and behaviour of the chromosomes and genes, the Mendelian Laws, sex determination, the endocrine functioning, the constitution and working of the sympathetic and parasympathetic systems, together with such various factors as climate, culture, tradition, social relationship and education. So for these reasons, *handwriting analysis is a discipline based also on intuition, that is to say, on an immediate insight by the graphologist into the handwriting as a whole.*

Many people object to the use of intuition but intuition enables us to press behind the appearance of life and thus to experience its essence. By means of reason we maintain our sanity and go about our daily activities, thinking mathematically in terms of time—past, present and future. But there is not only past, present and future—we are also in a space-time continuum. To deny this is to attempt to understand a motion picture by stopping the camera and studying the film, frame by frame. The meaning of the film is bound up with its motion. So it is that Geist can only be understood as a whole by the *intuitive* act resulting in insight.

In summary we may say that graphology is the science concerned with the analysis and interpretation of handwriting. Neurologically, it is a manifestation of brain functioning and here it should be noted that the hand (the usual prehensile extremity for handwriting) has a larger share of cortical representation within the brain than any other part or system of the body. Characterologically, it is a manifestation of psychic functioning. It is a science in that it possesses a body of organised knowledge derived from established findings in its field. It is a science, too, in that the established findings are the basis for the analysis of handwriting. Because of the subjective element inherent in all interpretation, graphology is not an exact science in the meaning that physics is but it must be remembered that *science is not limited to those areas of knowledge which can be interpreted only by purely objective methods involving exact measurement.* Moreover, the analytic findings have to be synthesised in order to produce a living whole, and this creative task is, of necessity, an art. Yet analysis and synthèsis are not two *separate* processes of mind, either in terms of functioning or in terms of time sequence, rather are they the polar aspects of all conceptualisation. From this it will be seen that the expert graphologist should have a knowledge of general psychology as well as a specialised knowledge of depth psychology and characterology. Additionally, he should have a broad cultural background covering the natural sciences, the social sciences and the humanities.

The basis of graphology can be reduced to strokes and curves which are expressed in the vertical or horizontal plane.* *Every stroke and curve, according to its plane, is an expression of 'I-to-Thou'.* Okakura said, 'Every single stroke of handwriting expresses a whole life.' This is the Parcelsian doctrine of 'Macrocosm-Microcosm' and it applies to the interpretation of handwriting. The expert graphologist, when he takes a single glance at a sample of handwriting, has an immediate insight into a whole. He has progressed beyond the stage of consciously reading the handwriting and is concerned only with interpretation which is derived from an unconscious analysis and synthesis of countless numbers of psychic polarities. *But everyone has intuition and as the student of graphology gains experience by comparing and contrasting samples of handwriting in the light of graphological theory, so will his powers of intuition develop accordingly.*

* And subtle differences of pressure must certainly be observed.

2 Character, Personality and Tests

When we speak of 'personality' we must recognise the difference between genuine and fictitious personality which is just as fundamental a difference as that between truth and falsehood. But what is 'personality'? And what is 'character'? Personality has been defined as how a man *appears* to other people. According to this definition, 'personality' cannot be the individual himself. It is not even a part of him and is therefore quite distinct from 'character' which is an integral part of the individual himself.

But what is the individual himself? Psychoanalysts have posited 'ego', 'super-ego' and 'id' and different approaches have been made by psychologists to the study of temperament and personality. But these methods, like all more or less orthodox methods of psychological procedure are becoming rule-of-thumb methods. They are becoming complicated mixtures of abstract theories and practical fallacies.

Tests have been devised to discover what kind of school work we should expect children to do at certain ages and what sort of education and training they should receive when they grow older. Thus psychologists began to substitute so-called scientific tests of children's mental abilities for the unscientific examinations generally used in former times and for the intuitive judgements of parents and teachers. As a matter of fact, many difficulties have arisen in the exact interpretation of the results of so-called intelligence tests. Moreover, in the meantime, it has been found that these tests have the great shortcoming that they cannot test character—the qualities of initiative, perseverance, determination, honesty, etc.—which it seems are more important in life and business than mere cleverness. Neither can they test the no-less-important quality of power-to-grasp-ideas. In their dilemma, psychologists began to invent methods of measuring personality and temperament. They have worked out (and are still working out) questionnaires. These questionnaires in most cases are intended to find out what a person has done or how he feels or thinks about different problems *but they certainly cannot give a clue about the character, personality or temperament of the testee.* Nevertheless, in spite of these and many other disadvantages, the questionnaire has been (and still is) widely used —especially in the U.S.A.—because, as Blackburn expressed it (PSYCHOLOGY AND THE SOCIAL PATTERN), 'little labour appears to be rewarded by relatively quick returns'. If one agrees with the definition that a man's personality is how he appears—or how he wants to appear—to other people, such a questionnaire might be useful to find out what a person desires to pretend or to simulate.

The Indians call this 'Maya'. 'Maya' means 'simulation' and is, they maintain, the very nature of the world-process. The more the simulation, the deeper, the more complex, the more real-seeming the world-process. In fact, *the more absurd and impossible the hypocrisy, the more real-seeming and, therefore, the deeper it deceives.* That, in essence, is the problem of personality.

Personality is not a something that can be grasped by studying and observing *the behaviour* of a person and also not by discovering *the various inborn traits of character.* Sociologists have added a new point. They emphasise the effects of culture on fashioning *the behaviour* of the individual. Certainly a sound objection but it does not really cover the problem of personality at all—it stresses the fact that the cultural influences may be of far more reaching importance than any innate characteristics.

But the question it, Does the conception of personality only imply *the behaviour-patterns* of an individual? There is no doubt that in the study of the human mind one cannot escape problems of *pattern* and *form.* When Goethe coined the term 'morphology' he was interested in the forms of flowers and skulls. And to this day, the term carries physical connotations. But the concept of morphology can be, to some extent, applied to the phenomena of behaviour. One could define morphology as the science of form. A dictionary tells us that form is the shape of anything as opposed to the substance of that thing. One can say that behaviour has shape. The shape which behaviour assumes has been investigated (and is investigated) in its own scientific right.

A morphological approach leads, therefore, to the description and *measurement of specific forms*, the systematic study of topographic relations and correlations of such forms and their ontogenic progressions and regressions, their comparative features among individuals and among species.

It was John Hunter who said, 'Structure is only the intimate expression of function.' In a monistic (*but not mystical*) sense, the mind has been regarded as a living, growing 'structure', even although it lacks corporeal tangibility. Some morphologists think that it is a complex, organising action-system which manifests itself in characteristic forms of behaviour—in patterns of posture, locomotion, prehension, manipulation, perception, communication, and social response. But this is all a little confusing. Yet of on thing we may be very clear—that the human mind is not as simple as many people (including psychologists) assume. *Nevertheless, it is the creed of the mental tester of today that in some way or other, and at some time or other, the most subtle mental processes and the most elusive mental products will be made amenable to measurements.* Thorndike expressed it concisely when he said, 'Everything exists in some amount and if it exists in some amount it can be measured'.

But does the mind exist in some amount? C. G. Ogden writes (A.B.C. OF PSYCHOLOGY), 'It is important to realise in spite of language, that the mind is not a thing but an activity. The images, ideas, etc. are not products but processes.' Is it really possible to measure ideas and images? We can measure sticks and stones, we can calculate the distance to the farthest stars *but we cannot fathom the depth of an emotion.* Nevertheless, there are people who have tried it, again and again and in vain.

As a matter of fact, nobody knows exactly what the mind really is. In the old days we heard of 'sensations', 'perceptions', 'imagination', 'judgement', 'aim', 'act-of-will' and 'feeling', that is to say, of the most elementary signs of mind and of the

CHARACTER, PERSONALITY AND TESTS

physical structure of our sensory organs.

One is taught how to draw conclusions, how to remember, how to form conceptions but concerning the riddles of personality, of temperament, of the study of the religious conscience, of the diseases of the soul or of the study of the practical facts of life, one has to agree with Klages when he said that one does not gain much more knowledge than the lover of flowers would gain from a study of botany when briefly instructed that plants are three-dimensional bodies, immobile, able to grow, requiring certain food and dependent on the light.

3 The Philosophical Basis of Graphology

As psychology became more 'scientific' it became more impoverished. The craze for measurement and for exactness swept over it. In order to become a respectable science psychology began to imitate the quantitative methods of the exact sciences and today the object of the exercise—the study of the psyche—has been lost behind a mass of neuro-physiological experiments and statistics.

But the mind cannot be studied apart from its philosophical aspects. And it seems to me that *the principle of polarity has to be applied to the study of all psychological processes.* Then, and only then, shall we understand why we are all such bundles of contradictions and why every human being is forced to choose the middle course between opposite extremes in any given time and place and circumstances. For our life is not merely the conscious and unconscious endeavour to keep balance between the spiritual and the demoniac tendencies, between Cain and Abel, between good and bad, between reality and illusion, between the masculine and the feminine tendencies. The world-process and the life-process is made up of infinite pairs of opposites, although they have to be regarded as aspects of the same. These pairs are always and inevitably inseparable but always one of the pair is more (and the other is less) in any given time, place or circumstances. For instance, there is no struggle for existence without alliance for existence—there is no parasitism without symbiosis. In a sense, each term of every pair is the other, is a continuation of the other, and yet is also different and opposite. Pleasure and sorrow, hope and despair, right and left, virtue and vice, day and night, man and woman are such pairs of opposites. Better expressed, all these are aspects

24

of the particular entity although they manifest themselves in opposite directions. One provokes the other in such a way that one cannot think of the day without the night, of the man without the woman, of virtue without vice, of hope without despair, etc. But despite this, one of the terms of any pair does not neutralise the other. Only the proportion of tension existing between the two opposites is variable. It may be increased or decreased, weakened or amplified but it can never be suspended or extinguished unless the entity in which the tension exists is itself annihilated. *And correlations of such opposed terms are called 'polarities'.*

From this point of view one cannot say that a man's personality is how he appears to other people. *Personality must be defined as the totality of all the bundles of contradictions in human nature;* of the 'persona' (the conscious and unconscious mask one shows to others); of character and temperament; of the reactions to environmental influences. *The character provokes the persona in such a way that one cannot think of the character without the persona.* And, of course, the persona never neutralises the character. It is the proportion of tension which is variable between these two poles of the total personality. The relationship between persona and character can be compared with the relationship between the two great forces in the universe, namely movement towards the centre (centripetal) and movement towards the periphery (centrifugal). The balance between them we term as negative and positive polarity. The centrifugal current from an electric cell is positive, the centripetal current is negative. Both are necessary to complete the circuit. It is hardly necessary to prove that the principle of polarity runs throughout nature. World and life is an eternal circuit—the pleasures of life and the terrors of death, the elixir of love and the venom of hate, flow through our senses together. We say one thing but we do another but it is always the one more at one time, then the other more at another time. But both are present at the same time. We are good and bad in the same moment and it is impossible to measure the good and the bad at any one moment. What we should be able to measure to some degree is the tension between the two opposites—the tension between the opposite aspects of the same entity we term 'total personality'.

Egocentricity is a movement towards the centre and sociality is a movement towards the periphery. *And I shall show how this principle of polarity is effective in one complex expression of the human mind, namely in the handwriting.* But this principle can be applied to other fields—muscular functioning (flexors opposed to extensors), conduct (moral behaviour opposed to immoral behaviour), the phenomena of the physical world (action opposed to reaction), etc.

But since everything in the world and life is composed of pairs of opposites and as all processes are ambivalent, it should be obvious that in the analysis of handwriting all characteristics must also be ambivalent. Just over a century ago, handwriting was regarded as a mosaic of signs placed side by side without inter-relation. It was for this reason that the interpretation of handwriting as an expression of character and personality proved to be largely a fallacy. *It is a fundamental error to suppose that each characteristic stands for a single property because every writing expression is ambivalent.* Moreover, one has to discriminate between genuine and fictitious expressions, between the genuine and the pseudo personality. But can we judge correctly at all? Do we really know our most intimate friends or do we only suppose we know them? Is anybody able to penetrate into the heart of his fellow being? It is true that we all possess two natures—of this there is no doubt—one we show and the other we conceal, one we pretend and the other we do not want to declare, one we present to society and one we present to our most intimate friends, with one we dream and with the other we act or we suffer. But both are intermingled parts of the same entity.

How may we detect in the ever-changing actions of man the permanent abiding characteristics? How may we detect his real motives behind the façade of his politeness or of his so-called good breeding? *How can we pierce and throw off the veils of Maya?*

We have to try to free ourselves of certain illusions. We suppose, erroneously, that each of us is craving for the truth but we are only interested in hunting for fresh illusions. We are swinging between hope and despair, between love and hate, between joy and sorrow, between pleasure and pain, between extroversion and introversion and so we grope about a labyrinth of polarities. And philosophers have tried again and again to find a way out from this maze we call life and world.

We have no idea about ourselves because *it is impossible for a person to be objective about himself*. If we seriously try to fathom ourselves or rather *imagine* that we are so doing we can see only a shadowy figure of ourselves, as in a glass darkly, as we were a moment ago, never as we are at the actual moment. *For our ego is always in the place from which it gazes outwards and never in the place to which its gaze is directed*. And though most of us will be unwilling to admit this conclusion (first made by Rudolph Allers in PSYCHOLOGY OF CHARACTER), yet we have to remember that this fundamental fact about the experiencing of self renders continuous self-knowledge impossible. For this reason our ultimate being, our 'total personality', must remain in the dark. We can, of course, gain some self-knowledge by recognition of certain data, providing us with terms of reference to something deeper. We can, of course, learn a lot about ourselves by self-observation. But if and when we seriously submit to self-observation, we become usually very puzzled, surprised and sometimes amazed. We realise then how little we know about ourselves. We realise then *that psychology is dealing not with facts but mostly with illusions*.

It has become obvious that many psychologists and characterologists who *think* they can solve the problems of mind, character and personality by testing and measuring are going astray. One feels compelled to avow that they are degrading themselves and their work by neglecting completely the philosophical aspects of their science. This is affirmed in spite of the fact that philosophy *alone* does not lead to practical results.

4 Historical Background to Graphology

Graphology as a science has a history of just under one hundred years. But the idea of a connection between handwriting and character/personality has existed since ancient times. Thus C. Suetonius Tranquillus, writing in A.D. 120 (DE VITA CAESARUM) observes, 'He does not hyphen the words and continue on to the following line, not even if this means cramming the letters, but simply squeezes them in and curves the end of the line downwards'. And in the fourth century A.D. the Chinese script called 'grass-writing' was already highly developed. Great store was set on handwriting by Kuo Jo-hsu (1060-1110 A.D.) when he remarked, 'Handwriting infallibly shows us whether it comes from a noble-minded or a vulgar person'. And it was Okakura who said, '*Every single stroke of handwriting expresses a whole life*'.

In Europe, in the early mediaeval period, handwriting was practised professionally by the monks. In the twelfth and thirteenth centuries, its use became more general among educated laymen due to the influence of Islamic culture. And its use became still more widespread through the influence of the Renaissance. The Renaissance researches of scholars also showed that Aristotle had had an interest in handwriting and personality and this was more than three hundred years before the birth of Christ.

Nearer our own times, the first published work on graphology appeared in Bologna at the beginning of the seventeenth century and was entitled IDEOGRAPHIA. This was followed, in 1622, by Camillo Baldi's detailed treatise, relating handwriting to personality. Baldi was a doctor and professor in the University of Bologna and his work had a suitably scholastic and lengthy title,

28

TRATTATO COME DA UNA LETTERA MASSIVA SI COGNOSCA LA NATURA E QUALITA DELLO SCRITORE. In this treatise he wrote, 'It is obvious that all persons write in their own peculiar way and that in private letters everybody uses such characteristic forms as cannot be truly imitated by anybody else'. And his conclusions were, 'These and other similar traits of character can be recognised in any handwriting by way of thorough examination. Yet it is necessary to observe carefully whether the characteristics of handwriting recur, moreover whether they are in any way artificial, and finally whether they result from various deceptive causes which are due to writing materials'. Jacoby has praised this work as 'the first step towards a science of graphology in Europe and, in fact, an admirably clever and lucid attempt'. Since that date, there have appeared many graphological works in different languages.

Leibniz, the German philosopher and mathematician, remarked, 'The manner of writing, as far as it does not follow that of the schoolmaster, expresses something of natural temperament'.

J. Ch. Grohmann, Professor of Theology and Philosophy at the University of Wittenberg, wrote (1792) a treatise entitled, EXAMINATION OF THE POSSIBILITY OF INFERRING CHARACTER FROM HANDWRITING. In this small work he observed, 'It is just as difficult to disguise one's handwriting as one's physiognomy. Just as the physiognomy remains fundamentally constant, and only the movable muscles are activated in contrast to the inner emotion, the character of the handwriting remains fundamentally the same in spite of all disguise, even if masked by assumed and deceptive traits. I have always found that the faculty of disguising the handwriting is on a level with that of disguising character and appearance'.

A brief and passing reference will suffice to the fact that the significance of handwriting was perceived by Gainsborough, Scott, Goethe, Lavater, Knigge and Stefan Zweig. There are observations on handwriting in the works of Browning, Poe, Sand, Humbolt, Baudelaire, Dumas, Daudet, Zola, Gogol, Chekhov, Heyse, Lombroso, Björnson, Kielland, Thomas Mann, Ludwig, Feuchtwanger, Hirschfeld, Kretschmer, Bleuler, Jung,

Einstein, etc.

It was *Michon*, the French abbé, who coined and introduced the term 'graphology', in 1871. He concentrated on studies of single letters, depending solely on empirical observation, thus lacking confirmation of his findings by way of psychological interpretation. *Crépieux-Jamin*, his pupil and successor, elaborated Michon's detailed observations, at the same time moving away from the 'school of fixed signs' to studies of the overall aspects of handwriting.

But it was *Preyer* (a child psychologist), *Meyer* (a psychiatrist) and *Klages* (a philosopher) who gave graphology a fresh impetus through their experimentation and psychological studies. More than any others, they have helped to place graphology on a sound basis with a claim to the status of a science. *Preyer* was a Professor of Physiology at the University of Jena and he demonstrated that a script produced by either left or right hand or foot, or even by the mouth, of the same person possessed a similarity of writing pattern. *Meyer* was a psychiatrist who stressed three important factors of writing movement—extension, speed and pressure. He helped to develop a new science of characterology because he recognised that problems of expression are aspects of character. It was *Klages* who developed a science of expression which postulated laws and principles governing graphology, expressive movement and characterology. He also taught that the basic law of expression is that each expressive physical movement actualises the tensions and drives of the personality. *He stressed the importance of assessing by intuition the rhythm of a script and so arriving at the 'form level'.* *Kraepelin* was a psychiatrist who devised the 'Kraepelin Scale' which attempts to measure writing speed and pressure in the scripts of both the mentally well and unwell.

Attempts have been made to separate graphology from any particular philosophical orientation in characterology and to base it firmly on the findings and teachings of one of the schools of depth psychology—Freudian psychoanalysis, Jungian Analytical Psychology, Adlerian Individual Psychology, Szondian Schicksalpsychology, etc. *Schlag* and *Pulver* (the Swiss graphologist) made such attempts within the framework of Jung's system. In particular, it was Pulver who has reduced the entire theories and teachings of graphology to the formula: *'Writing is the path leading from the "I" to the "You"; it is the bridge over which the communication moves from the "Ego" to the "environment"'*. A Freudian-orientated graphologist might phrase it similarly by stating that *'Writing is the symbolism that expresses the underlying ego-object relationships'*. In Freudian theory, everybody and everything (the so-called 'environment') are the 'objects' which the 'ego' 'cathects' (i.e. invests) with 'libido' (psycho-sexual energy). Additionally, it must be mentioned that Pulver has studied the symbolism of the writing space.

A graphological journal was launched in 1939 by three Czech graphologists: *Fanta, Menzel* and *Schönfeld*. There had been other graphological journals previously—Klages had founded and edited the ZENTRALBLATT FUER GRAPHOLOGIE (the supplement to his ZEITSCHRIFT FUER MENSCHENKUNDE)—but the short-lived nature of this Czech periodical was much to be regretted.

In Hungary a graphological institute was established in 1920. Notable among Hungarian graphologists have been *Roman, Balazs* and *Hajnal*. Graphology has received official recognition in Hungary because university psychologists as well as clinicians supplement their findings, researches and techniques by graphological findings, researches and techniques. And applied graphology has found an outlet in Hungarian educational research. Roman devised a 'graphodyne' for measuring graphological phenomena while Balaz and Hajnal studied the subject in terms of psychoanalysis.

In the U.S.A., graphology has received the attention of *June Downey* of the University of Iowa, as well as of *Allport* and *Vernon* of the Harvard Psychological Clinic. In her researches, Downey used the matching method, comparing judgements based on handwriting with findings based on gesture, gait, carriage, etc. Allport and Vernon, however, made more use of statistics and the experimental approach. Mention can be made here of *Saudek*, a Czech graphologist, who attempted to deal with graphological problems in terms acceptable to the experimental psychologists. He worked in collaboration with Allport and Vernon. An important conclusion of the experimental psychologists and their collaborating graphologists was *the experimental confirmation that an isolated trait, as such, has no fixed meaning.* A more clinical approach, making use of scales, has been made by *Zubin* and *Lewinson* and this was followed up by the work of *Rose Wolfson.* *Wolff* is investigating contemporary experimental graphology and *Sonnemann* investigated contemporary clinical graphology.

In Switzerland, there was *Pulver* whose name and work have already been mentioned. There was also *Heider* who in 1941 published his EXAKTE GRAPHOLOGIE. Heider's researches and conclusions are so important that I propose to comment briefly on them here.

In studying the pressure of the hand and of the little finger on the writing surface, it was Saudek who found that this particular pressure produces an unintentional shifting of the writing-paper during the act of writing. But it was Heider who argued that this pressure of the hand, though not consciously intentional, is caused by bipolar psychic energies and has something to do with what he calls 'the weight' of a handwriting. He was impressed by the discovery that every person, male or female, produces both masculine and feminine hormones with either the masculine or the feminine hormones predominating. He supposed that masculine and feminine energies constitute the psyche of a person and that everybody produces masculine and feminine energies at the same time but with the masculine or the feminine predominating. He brought these energies into correlation with the size and width of a handwriting and with the pressure of the hand which causes the unintentional shifting of the paper. As the size and expansion of written letters and words depends upon the way of shifting the paper during the act of writing, Heider assumed that the pressure of the hand and of the little finger is caused by the psychic energies. *Masculine energies* produce a large and wide writing, *feminine energies* a small and narrow writing. *The actual sex* of a person does not matter. He based his theories on the concept that handwriting is the result of the laying-on of multitudes of minute particles of ink (in the case of a pen) or of graphite (in the case of a pencil). In the light of this, some common observations acquire a new significance. For instance, after somebody has used a pen for a reasonable length of time it can be observed that one side of the nib has been worn down more than the other. In other words, we unconsciously concentrate the writing pressure either on the left side or on the right side of the nib. This preference is so definite that pen manufacturers produce left-oblique and right-oblique nibs. Now a pressure on the left point of the nib results in a spraying of minute ink particles from left to right—*a clockwise movement*. But a pressure on the right point of the nib produces a spraying of minute particles of ink from right to left—*an anti-clockwise movement*. These movements constitute what Heider called the '*internal writing flow*' of a script, the direction of which is only in accordance with the left-to-right movements in European writings if the pressure on the left side of the pen or pencil is emphasised. A clockwise internal flow, regarded from the starting point on the left side of every written unit, has tendencies to the right. An anti-clockwise internal flow turns into the direction from which the writing movement emerges. This is a mechanical phenomenon yet it is also of great consequence for the psychological interpretation of handwriting. For Freudian graphologists, it opens new vistas for research into ego-object relationships. Heider's own *psychological* conclusions I cannot accept. Being an electrical engineer and physicist, he developed a rigid, logical and mechanistic psychological system from his findings but *behaviour is basically instinctual and emotional and therefore lacks logic which is a secondary process phenomenon* (see page 39).

In England, graphology has made little impression and still less progress, in the past. This is due to the conservativeness of the English mind—it is worth remembering that it has taken Freudian psychoanalysis nearly sixty years to achieve its present-day measure of currency and acceptance in England. But there are now favourable and hopeful indications that, as with psychoanalysis, there is a change of climate suitable for the fuller acceptance and further development of graphology. Saudek (the Czech graphologist) lived for a time in England and made important contributions (acceptable to Allport and Vernon) on the mechanics of handwriting—and his researches were popularised by Brooks for English-speaking readers. *Jacoby* also lived for a time in England and it was in this country that he wrote his influential and fundamental text, ANALYSIS OF HANDWRITING. He was a brilliant graphologist whose untimely death was a great loss to our science. *Singer* also came to live in England and here wrote his books and carried on with his practice. And *Strelisker* came to England in 1939 and carried on his teaching, research and practice until his death, in 1962. His post-1934 researches have not yet been published and since his published work appeared between 1931 and 1934 graphologists are not aware of his later researches into the work of Heider, the Swiss graphologist.

In Germany, graphology has had a more favourable and welcome reception. It always forms an integral part of every psychology course and indeed a degree can be taken at a number of universities. There is *Heiss* who is Professor of Psychology and Characterology (and Director of the Institute of Psychology and Characterology) at the University of Freiburg-im-Breisgau, South Germany. There is *Pophal* who was appointed Professor of Neurology at the University of Hamburg. There is *Bürger* who was Professor of Medicine at the University of Leipzig and who treated graphology with respect in his DIE HAND DES KRANKEN. And, amongst others, there are *Wittlich*, *Müller* and *Enskatt*— the two latter are lecturers at the University of West Berlin.

There are of course many names who have contributed (and still are contributing) to graphological science. If I have mentioned but a few so far, it is because of reasons of space and not because of any prejudices on my part. For fuller information I must refer the reader to the bibliography at the end of this book which lists one hundred and fifty titles, a personal selection I made from a bibliography of more than six hundred titles. And sound graphological teaching has also been transmitted orally by teachers who have never written a line on the subject. Like many criminals who have never appeared in the dock, there are many graphologists who have never appeared in print.

What your handwriting reveals

What your handwriting reveals

What your handwriting reveals

What your handwriting reveals

What your handwriting reveals

What your handwriting reveals

What your handwriting reveals

What your handwriting reveals

What your handwriting reveals

What your handwriting reveals

What your handwriting reveals

What your handwriting reveals

What your handwriting reveals

What your handwriting reveals

What your handwriting reveals.

What you handwriting reveals

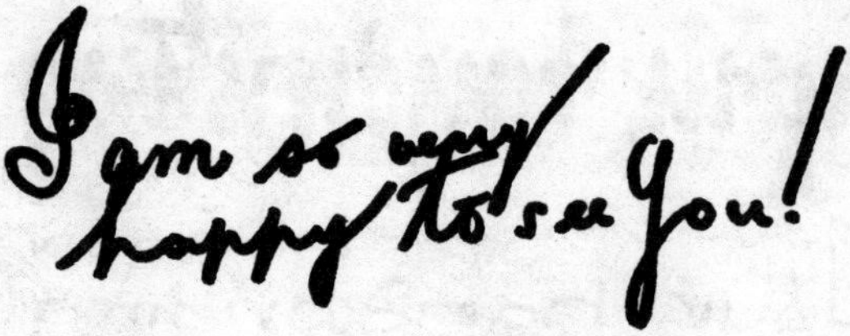

Fig. 1.   Poor standard of form-level

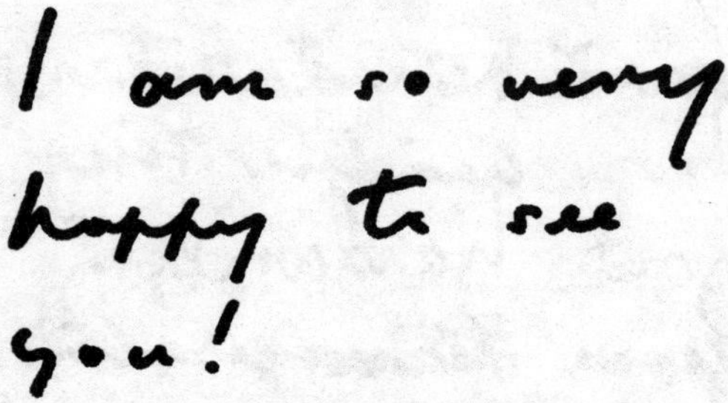

Fig. 2.   Good standard of form-level

5 Form-Level

The doctrine of form-level owes its origin and development to Ludwig Klages. Mention of his contributions to the establishment of graphology as a scientific discipline and its further developments has already been made in another section of this book.

The findings of Meyer, Preyer and Erlenmeyer were combined and further developed by Klages into his 'science of expression'. He taught that there is correspondence between different aspects of movement—facial expression, speech and handwriting. They have a common 'form-level' which is evaluated according to the 'rhythm' of the individual's movement. *And 'rhythm', according to Klages, is something indefinable which can only be understood by 'intuition'.* Thus the form-level of a script is the basic criterion of its qualities as a whole. *So before any examination of single features in a script is undertaken, the sample as a whole should be examined in order to determine its form-level.* If the form-level is evaluated as 'above average', then the positive aspects of the individual's characteristics are chosen. If the form-level is evaluated as 'below average', then the negative aspects of the individual's characteristics are chosen. If the form-level is evaluated as 'average', then both poles of each characteristic have to be brought into consideration in order to determine which of the two poles—however slight the degree of polarisation—is the more appropriate interpretation. There may be also ambivalence—the simultaneous presence of both poles and in equal intensity.

Klages' doctrine of the form-level has been largely accepted by the German school of graphologists but has been much criticised and largely rejected by graphologists outside of the German cultural orbit. But if the thesis is accepted that graphology is a Geisteswissenschaft—as I maintain—then such criticisms and rejection constitute a complete misunderstanding, as well as a serious loss to graphological development. It is true that Klages' style of writing is heavy and involved—but this is no more than a normally accepted characteristic of some German-speaking scholars—but much of the criticism is not only uninformed, it is personal and prejudiced. It is said that his writings are understood by few, presumably the critics count themselves among the elect in their understanding! Roman agrees with Kroeber-Keneth who stigmatised the intangible phenomenon of rhythm as an unacceptable procedure in these words '. . . the evaluation of yesterday' (DIE LESERLICHKEIT DER HANDSCHRIFT in vol. XII, nos. 4-5, 1935, of INDUSTRIELLE PSYCHOTECHNIK). Again she accepts the judgement of Angyal when he writes that Klages' theory 'exaggerates the conflict between what he calls "Geist" (conscious mental function, spirit) and "Seele" (feeling life, soul). The two are, for him, antagonistic forces. The "Geist", according to Klages, penetrates from outside into life like a wedge, causing ... a fundamental split ... Klages ... regards the mind as a factor which disturbs living, as a "Lebensstörung"' (FOUNDATIONS FOR A SCIENCE OF PERSONALITY, New York, 1941).

I do not propose to be drawn too much into the fun-and-games of metaphysics nor to engage in a gigantic play of words but I must, nonetheless, make the following comments.

These criticisms of the role of intuition, quoted by Roman, ignore the views of Bergson, the eminent French philosopher, who made a fundamental distinction between 'time' (a mathematical concept of the atomistic thinking of the intellect) and 'duration' (a metaphysical concept appropriate to the holistic insights of intuition). Mathematical and rational thinking by the intellect enables us to go about our daily business and to preserve our sanity by stopping the flow of life, so to speak, and concerning ourselves with the static reproduction with each individual aspect of that stream. But it is the stream or motion alone that gives life its meaning or configuration—in a word, its 'Gestalt'. And the meaning or Gestalt can only be *understood by intuition*.

Again, when Klages uses the words 'Geist' and 'Seele', he is using them in opposition to each other—indeed the title of his
38

most important work is DER GEIST ALS WIDERSACHER DER
SEELE (THE GEIST AS CONTRADICTION/OPPONENT OF THE SEELE).
In this context, 'Geist' can be translated as 'conscious mind' and
'Seele' can be translated as 'instinctual life' (see page 100).
If we pursue this polarity of 'Geist' and 'Seele' within the con-
ceptual framework of Freudian psychoanalysis we can see that
under 'Geist' we may list:

(a) 'secondary processes' which obey the laws of grammar and
formal logic, use bound instinctual energies, and are governed
by the 'reality principle';
(b) the 'reality principle' which reduces the unpleasure of instinctual tensions by adaptive behaviour;
(c) 'the ego' which is that part of the 'id' which has been modi-
fied by the direct influence of the external world;
(d) 'secondary repression' which completes the task of 'primary
repression' in that derivatives and disguised manifestations
of unacceptable instinctual impulses are kept unconscious;
(e) 'sublimation' which is the developmental process by which
instinctual energies are discharged in those non-instinctual
forms of behaviour which we call 'culture'.

And under 'Seele' we may list:

(a) 'primary processes' which are characteristic of unconscious
mental activity, which ignore the laws of grammar and
formal logic, use unbound instinctual energies, and are
governed by the 'pleasure principle';
(b) the 'pleasure principle' which reduces the unpleasure of
instinctual tensions by immediate activity regardless of
reality considerations;
(c) the 'id' which 'contains everything that is present at birth,
that is fixed in the constitution—above all, therefore, the
instincts, which originate from the somatic organisation and
which find a first psychical expression here (in the id) in
forms unknown to us'—Freud (1940);
(d) 'primary repression' by which the initial emergence of an
unacceptable impulse is prevented;
(e) 'instinctual discharges' accompanied by 'instinctual satisfac-

39

tion' resulting from the emotions experienced as instinctual tensions are reduced regardless of reality considerations.

From a comparison of the Freudian concepts listed under 'Geist' it will be evident that the development of 'mind' is fundamentally in opposition to the undisturbed expression of 'life' In this sense, 'mind' ('Geist') is indeed a factor which disturbes 'living' ('Seele')—it is a 'Lebensstörrung' ('an inhibiting and distracting influence to living'). *Therefore, in this sense, Klages is correct.* Concerning Klages' further metaphysical speculations we need not concern ourselves here. He has demonstrated the importance of 'polarity', of intuition and holism. He has also emphasised what is the classical psychoanalytical view that *'mind' has its origin and development in 'stress'.* The fact that an optimal or minimal quantum of 'stress' is a necessity of life does not invalidate Klages' theory that the beginning of 'Geist' is also the beginning of 'stress', of 'Lebensstörrung'.

But for practical purposes we assess the quality of the form-level by a consideration of:

(a) the originality of the script (see page 71)
(b) the naturalness or artificiality of the script (see pages 71, 89)
(c) the distribution of spaces. (See page 59.)

As a result of these considerations the quality of the form-level is determined as being:

(a) above average
(b) average
(c) below average.

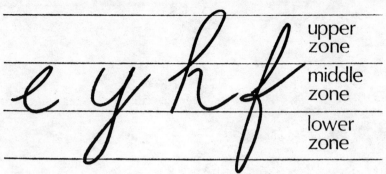

upper
zone

middle
zone

lower
zone

Fig. 3. The zones of a script

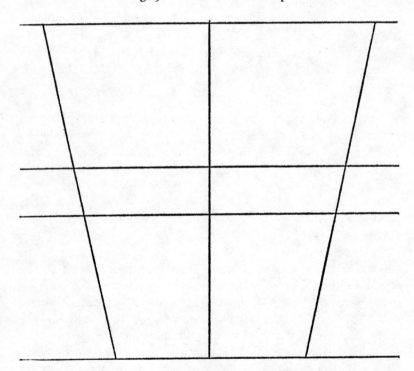

Control	Distance	Relaxation
Inhibition	Independence	Spontaneity
Egocentricity	Neutrality	Sociality
Introversion	Self-	Extroversion
Conservativeness	sufficiency	Radicalism

Fig. 4. The direction of a script

6 The Directions and Zones of Handwriting

Handwriting moves in both the horizontal and the vertical planes. In the horizontal plane there are three directions: leftwards or backwards, upright or vertical, rightwards or forwards. In the vertical plane there are three zones: the upper, the middle, the lower.

Letters containing upper lengths which extend into the upper zone are: 'b', 'd', 'h', 'k', 'l', 't' as well as all capitals. Letters which are limited to the middle zone are 'a', 'c', 'e', 'm', 'n', 'o', 'r', 's', 'u', 'v', 'w', 'x'. Letters containing lower lengths which extend into the lower zone are: 'g', 'j', 'p', 'q', 'y', 'z'. Only the letter 'f' occupies all three zones; every letter constitutes part of the middle zone. The upper zone letters also constitute part of the middle zone, as do also the lower zone letters.

It must be remembered that handwriting is the path leading from the 'I' to the 'You', as Pulver said. As the Freudians would say, it symbolises the relationship of the ego to its objects (environment). Therefore, every forward or rightward impulse of the writer expresses his desire to reach out from himself to the world and life. The more his writing leans forward, the more he extroverts. The more his writing approximates to the perpendicular, the less willing is he to reach out to world and life. And the more his writing leans backward, the more he introverts—he is then unwilling to reach out to world and life. The forward-sloping writer is the extrovert who is concerned with the outer world in which he wants to make his impression on people and things. The backward-sloping writer is the introvert who is concerned with the inner world of thoughts and feelings and visions. The perpendicular writer is a neutral with moderate degrees of extroversion and introversion in his make-up. And if a writer oscillates between forward-sloping and backward-sloping script he is ambivalent in his attitudes to world and life; should he oscillate even within a single word, his ambivalence is still more pronounced. Of course, no writing is absolutely sloping in one particular direction. *What is sought is the overall, predominant slope.*

When the writing instrument moves into the upper zone, this is effected by means of the extensor muscles. This is a movement away from the writer's body and symbolises a psychological sphere of reflection and meditation, of abstraction and speculation—one that is unfettered by material considerations. But when the writing instrument moves into the lower zone, this is effected by means of the flexor muscles. And this is a movement towards the writer's body and symbolises a psychological sphere of primitive instinct and materiality, of irrationality. It should be noted, too, that whereas the flexor movements are accompanied by feeling tones of pleasure, the extensor movements are primarily accompanied by feeling tones of unpleasure. Between the upper and the lower zones is the middle zone and this symbolises the balance between the cultural and the instinctual spheres of personality, the dynamic equilibrium, the practical adjustment demanded of every living organism. The geometry book says that the shortest distance between any two points is a straight line *but a script consisting of one straight line would be meaningless as a communication* and we would conclude that the writer's mind had also become meaningless—in other words that he was in a state of de-personalisation, of psychosis. So some detouring into the upper and lower zones (although strictly and theoretically speaking a sign of unwillingness to progress, to communicate, to extrovert) is necessary if our communication is to be meaningful. Again, the extreme theoretical axiom of the shortest distance between two points being the straight line would suggest that extreme extroversion is the solution. But extreme extroversion, *extreme rightward-sloping handwriting, would coincide with the straight line which would be quite meaningless as a communication from the 'I' to the 'Thou'.* And such extreme extroversion (like the extreme use of the middle zone flattened to the thickness of a tape worm) would indicate the meaninglessness of the extreme extrovert's mind. These remarks apply equally to extreme leftward-sloping writing, to extreme introversion. Written language recognises this in that the letters of the alphabet permit the writer to express his meaning more clearly by extensions into both the upper and the lower zones. It should be mentioned, too, that thready writing can be diagnostic of nervous excitability, of low resistance, of indecision, of hysteria. And in Hitler's signature, the letters topple over each other towards the right, thus attempting to achieve *the theoretical straight line of a meaningless communication.*

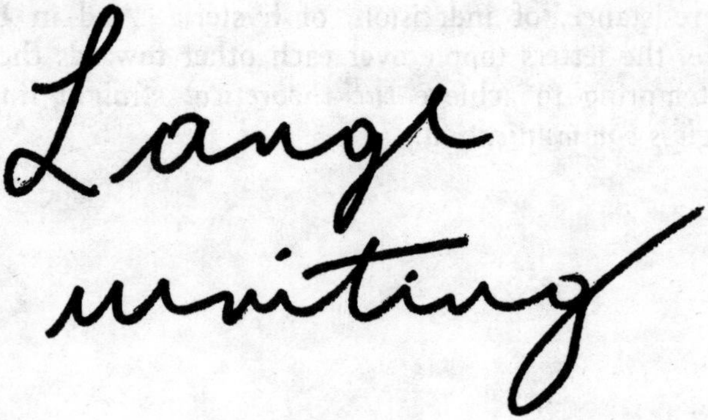

Fig. 5.   Size: large writing

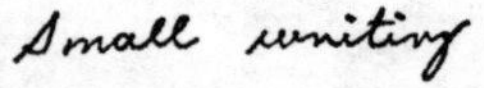

Fig. 6.   Size: small writing

7 Size of Script

The size of a script symbolises fundamentally the writer's assessment of himself.

It is evaluated out of the size of the small letters—⅛ inch or 3 mm. is the normal size.

A large script can be interpreted positively as superiority, seriousness, pride, generosity.

It can be interpreted negatively as arrogance, conceit, pomp, boastfulness.

A small script can be interpreted positively as devotion, respectfulness, humility, tolerance.

It can be interpreted negatively as inferiority feelings, faint-heartedness, lack of self-confidence, fear.

Fig. 7.   Right-slant

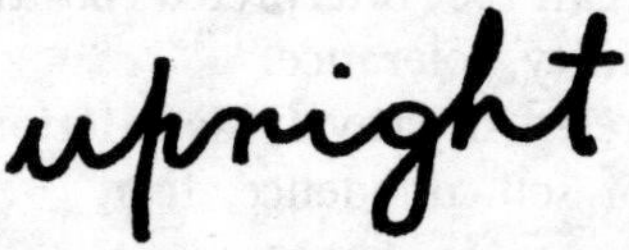

Fig. 8.   Vertical or upright slant

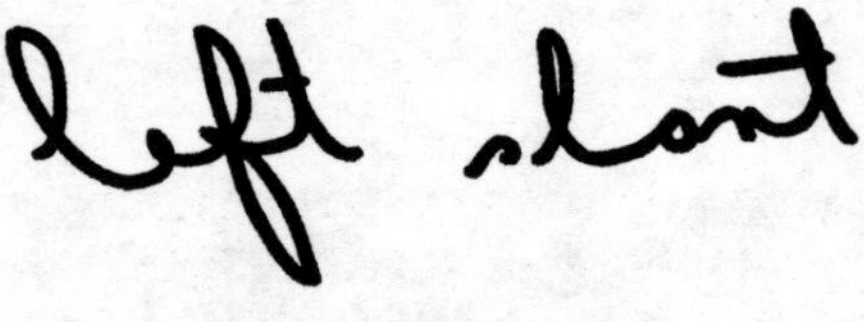

Fig. 9.   Left-slant

8 Slant or Writing-Angle

There are three main slants or writing-angles:

(a) Right-slant
(b) Upright
(c) Left-slant

The right-slant symbolises extroversion and progression, an outward movement towards world and life.

The upright script symbolises distance and self-sufficiency as far as world and life are concerned.

The left-slant symbolises introversion and regression, an inward movement towards the ego, away from world and life.

The right-slanting script (with a writing-angle of 95-145 degrees) can be interpreted positively as activity, sympathy, sociability or expressiveness.

Negatively it can be interpreted as restlessness, haste, immoderateness or hysteria.

The upright script (with a writing-angle of 85-95 degrees) can be interpreted positively as neutrality, dominance of reason, self-control or reserve.

Negatively it can be interpreted as egotism, lack of pity, coldness or rigidity.

The left-slanting script (with a writing-angle of less than 85 degrees) can be interpreted positively as self-denial, self-control, reserve or conservative-mindedness.

Negatively it can be interpreted as affectation, egotism, withdrawal or fear of the future.

A right-slanting script with a writing angle of more than 145 degrees should be interpreted negatively, so should a left-slanting script with a writing-angle of less than 60 degrees.

Fig. 10.   Narrow script

Fig. 11.   Wide script

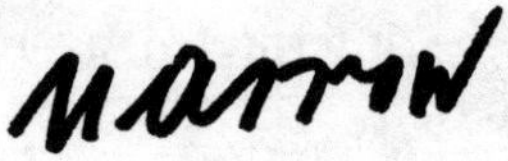

Fig. 12.   Narrow script

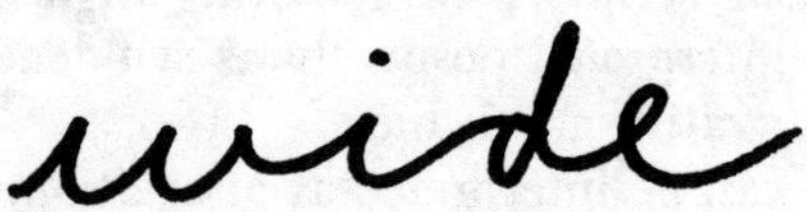

Fig. 13.   Wide script

9 Width and Narrowness

In a wide writing the distance between the downstrokes of small letters is greater than the height.

In a normal writing the distance between the downstrokes of small letters is equal to the height.

In a narrow writing the distance between the downstrokes of small letters is less than the height.

Wide writing symbolises extroversion, a centrifugal (outward) movement towards society, world and life. There can be *élan* and expansion, sympathy and vivacity. There are no inhibitions in personal relationships.

A *narrow writing symbolises introversion*, a centripetal (inward) movement towards the ego. There can be inhibition or self-control, modesty or timidity. There are inhibitions in personal relationships.

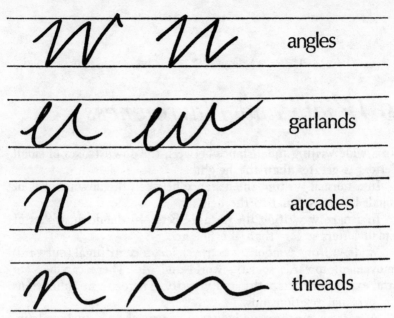

angles

garlands

arcades

threads

Fig. 14. Forms of connection

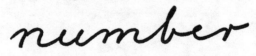

Fig. 15. Angular script

Fig. 16. Garland script

Fig. 17. Arcade script

Fig. 18. Thready script

10 Connections

The form of connection is of central importance. Connection means the manner in which the upstrokes and downstrokes of the letters of the middle zone are joined by means of curves or angles. It is the decisive form in the middle zone, constituting the actual centre of the writing movement form the 'I' to the 'You'. From the form of connection we learn about the writer's ability to adjust or to adapt to work, society and life. *It is also the most difficult to disguise of all writing features* and is therefore of great importance in the investigation of forgeries.

There are four main types of connection:

(a) angle
(b) garland
(c) arcade
(d) thread

The angular form of connection symbolises resistance.
Positively it can be interpreted as stability, persistence, energy or sincerity.
Negatively it can be interpreted as rigidity, hardness, stubbornness or quarrelsomeness.
The garland form of connection symbolises naturalness.
Positively it can be interpreted as frankness, sociability, hospitality or approachability.
Negatively it can be interpreted as fickleness, dependency, irresolution or laziness.
The arcade form of connection symbolises reserve.
Positively it can be interpreted as diplomacy, distance, scepticism or taciturnity.
Negatively it can be interpreted as artificiality, mendacity, closeness or scheming.

53

CONNECTIONS

The thready form of connection symbolises emotional lability.
Positively it can be interpreted as psychological talent, excitability, flexibility or versatility.

Negatively it can be interpreted as hysteria, cunning, mimicry or elusiveness.

NOTES

Fig. 19. Connected script

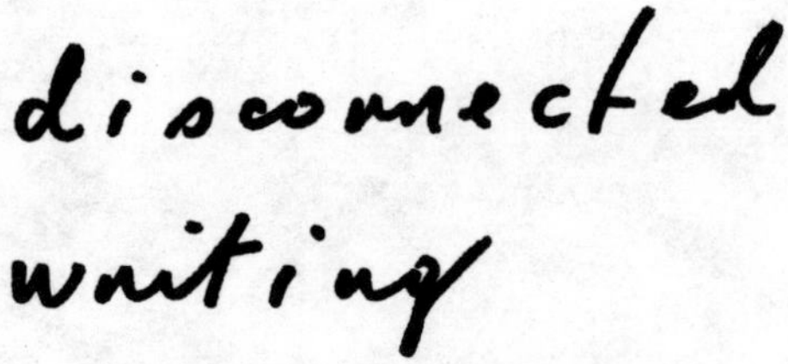

Fig. 20. Disconnected script

11 Connectedness

Connectedness shows to what extent adaptation has been achieved. It indicates the actual and social fitting of the writer into the environment. *It is also the criterion of his ability to engage in consequential thinking.*

A connected script is one in which five or more letters are written in one stroke. Breaks in the script caused by the dotting of a letter 'i' or the crossing of a letter 't' do not count.

A disconnected script is one in which four or less letters are written in one stroke. Type script is not a disconnected script.

A connected script can be interpreted positively as consequential thinking, co-operativeness, task perseverance or reproductive intelligence.

Negatively it can be interrupted as overadaptability, mass-mindedness, poverty of ideas or flightiness.

A disconnected script can be interpreted positively as intuitive thinking, self-reliance, individualism or productive observation.

Negatively it can be interpreted as egocentricity, mental jumpiness, inconsistency or loneliness.

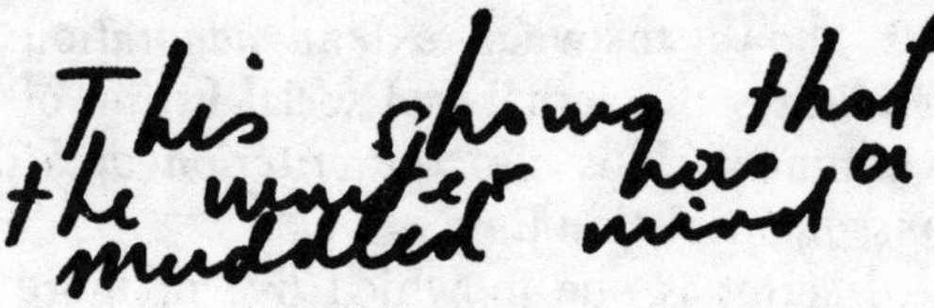

This shows that
the writer has a
muddled mind

Fig. 21. Poor spacing

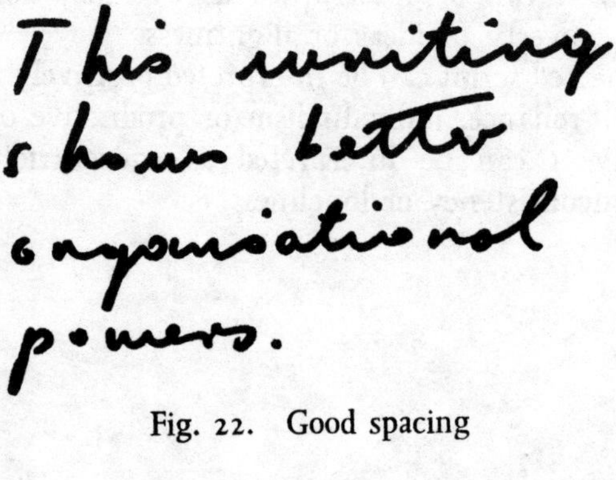

This writing
shows better
organisational
powers.

Fig. 22. Good spacing

12 Space Distribution between Words and Lines

Space distribution between words and lines symbolises organisational abilities.

A wide script can be interpreted positively as formality, orderliness in thinking, generosity or creative ability.

Negatively it can be interpreted as lack of spontaneity, lavishness, isolation or inconsiderateness.

A narrow distribution can be interpreted positively as spontaneity, economy, informality or instinctual thinking.

Negatively it can be interpreted as impulsiveness, avarice, familiarity or confused thinking.

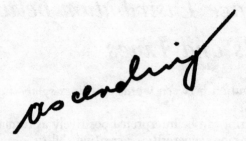

Fig. 23.   Direction of lines: ascending

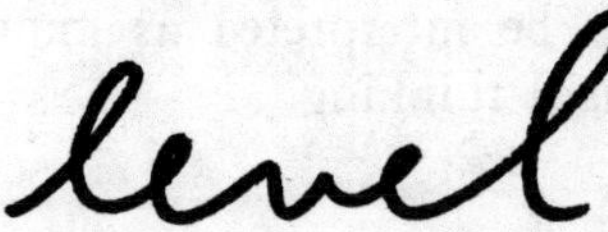

Fig. 24.   Direction of lines: level or horizontal

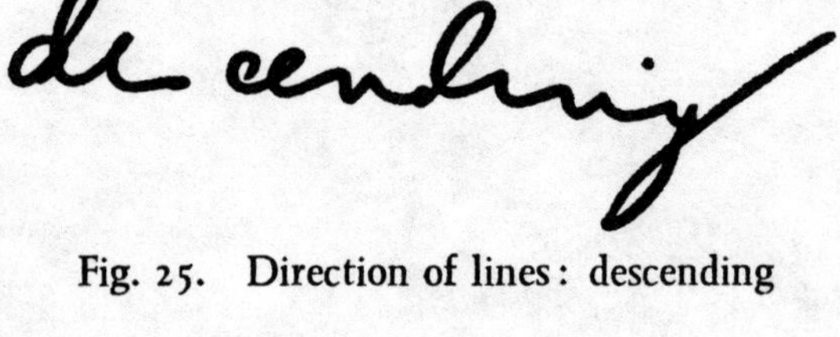

Fig. 25.   Direction of lines: descending

13 Direction of Lines

Lines of a script may be predominantly straight horizontal, ascending or descending in their direction.

The direction of lines symbolises moods which may be purely of the moment or they may be of longer duration. Therefore, if there is only one sample of handwriting available for analysis, it is safer to omit any evaluation based on the direction of lines, unless there is strong supporting evidence from the sample as a whole.

Ascending lines may be interpreted positively as ambition, optimism, zeal or single-mindedness.

Negatively they can be interpreted as anger, lack of a sense of reality, frivolity or restlessness.

Descending lines may be interpreted positively as depression, fatigue, pessimism or hypersensitivity.

Negatively they can be interpreted as exhaustion, lack of will, illness or suicidal tendencies.

Straight lines may be interpreted positively as methodicalness, constancy, perseverance or emotional control.

Negatively they may be interpreted as pedantry, poker-face, dullness or rigidity.

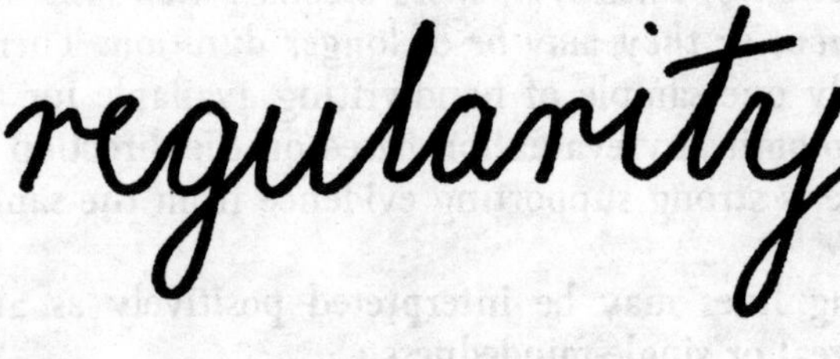

regularity

Fig. 26.   Regular writing

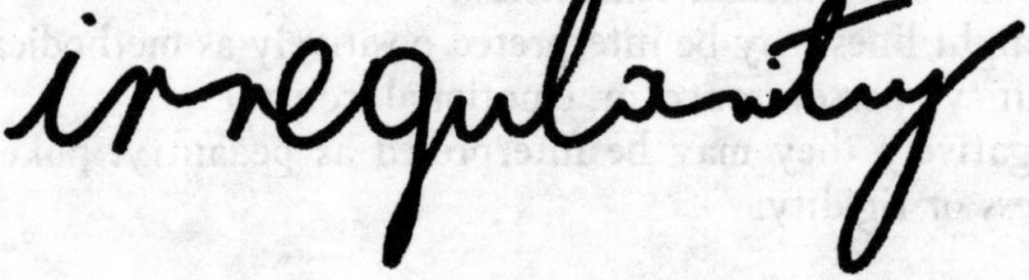

irregularity

Fig. 27.   Irregular writing

14 Regularity and Irregularity

Regularity of script symbolises control.
It is determined by:

(a) the regularity of the height of downstrokes in the middle zone
(b) the regularity of the height and the distance of downstrokes in the middle zone
(c) the regularity of slant.

Regularity can be interpreted positively as self-conquest, resistance, harmony, moderation.

It can be interpreted negatively as coldness, dullness, stereotypy, indifference.

Irregularity of script symbolises emotionality.

Irregularity can be interpreted positively as impulsivity, warmth, creativity, impressionability.

It can be interpreted negatively as moodiness, irritability, capriciousness, excitability.

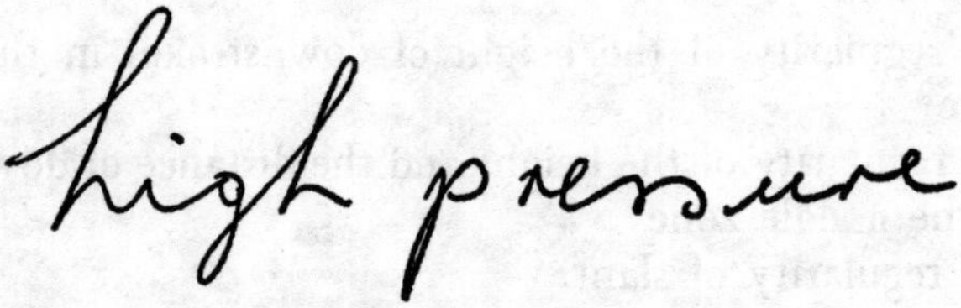

high pressure

Fig. 28. High pressure

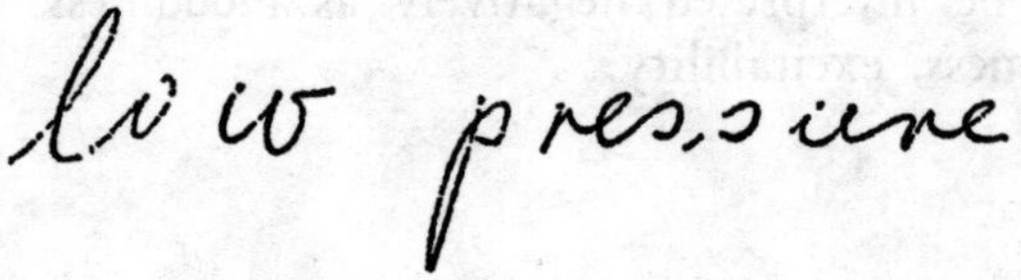

low pressure

Fig. 29. Low pressure

15 Pressure

High pressure in combination with a regular script symbolises will power.

It can be interpreted positively as tenacity, reliability, energy, self-control.

Negatively it can be interpreted as vanity, clumsiness, heaviness, stubbornness.

High pressure in combination with an irregular script symbolises emotionality.

It can be interpreted positively as adaptability, receptivity, vitality, impulsiveness.

Negatively it can be interpreted as aggressiveness, brutality, irritability, excitability.

Low pressure in combination with a regular script symbolises adaptability.

It can be interpreted positively as modesty, agility, mobility, femininity.

Negatively it can be interpreted as lack of initiative, lack of energy, yieldingness, unsteadiness.

Low pressure in combination with an irregular script symbolises receptivity.

Positively it can be interpreted as idealism, dreaminess, impressionability, sensitivity.

Negatively it can be interpreted as timidity, weakness, liability, superficiality.

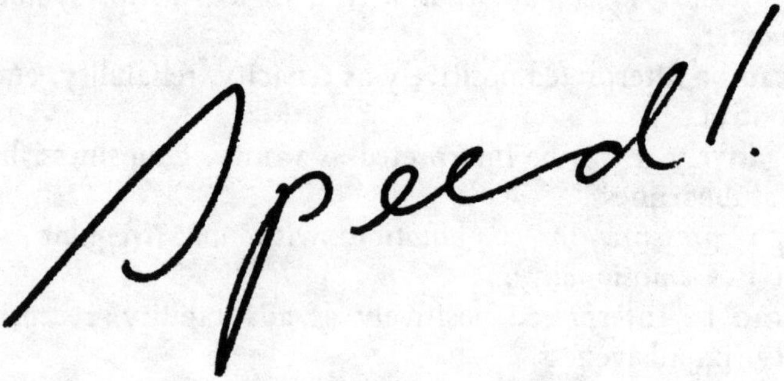

Speed!

Fig. 30.   Speed

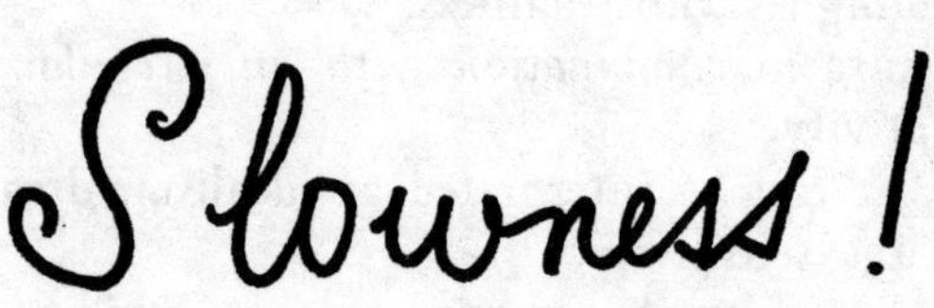

Slowness!

Fig. 31.   Slowness

16 Speed

A speedy script can be interpreted positively as spontaneity, generosity, extroversion, self-confidence.

Negatively it may be interpreted as aimlessness, flightiness, cockiness, rashness.

A slow script can be interpreted positively as considerateness, caution, steadiness, introversion.

Negatively it may be interpreted as laziness, hesitancy, insincerity, inactivity.

Speed is determined by:

(a) incompletion of final letters of words
(b) garland or thready connection
(c) 'i'-dots and 't'-bars omitted or placed to the right
(d) originality
(e) naturalness
(f) good distribution of spaces
(g) simplification
(h) connectedness
(i) wide script
(j) ascending lines
(k) predominance of right moving tendencies
(l) right slant
(m) large script
(n) even pressure

Slowness is determined by:

(a) completion of terminal letters of words
(b) angular connection
(c) 'i'-dots and 't'-bars placed above or to the left
(d) lack of originality

67

SPEED

(e) artificiality
(f) poor distribution of spaces
(g) ornamentation, elaboration, flourishes
(h) disconnectedness
(i) narrow script
(j) descending lines
(k) predominance of left tending movements
(l) left slant
(m) small script
(n) uneven pressure

NOTES

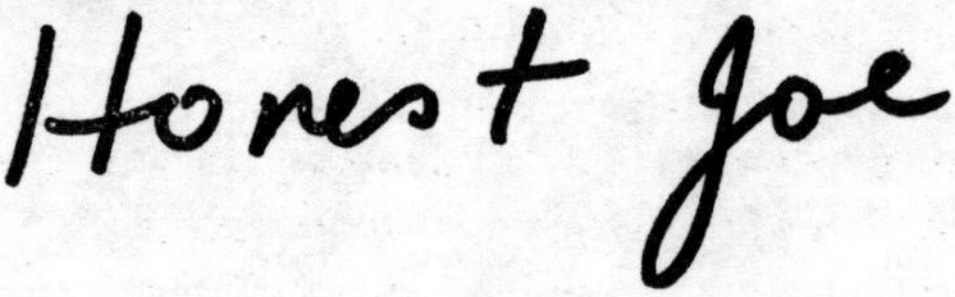

Honest Joe

Fig. 32.   Simplification

Fig. 33.   Ornamentation

17 Ornamentation and Simplification

Ornamentation consists of additions or flourishes which are not prescribed by the copy-book pattern.

Simplification—*not to be identified with leanness*—consists of reduced basic letter forms which still retain their legibility.

Ornamentation can be interpreted positively as originality, form sense, creativeness, pride.

Negatively it can be interpreted as affection, vulgarity, vanity, insincerity.

Simplification can be interpreted positively as maturity, simplicity, essentiality, orderliness.

Negatively it can be interpreted as lack of form sense, unreliability, tactlessness, insincerity.

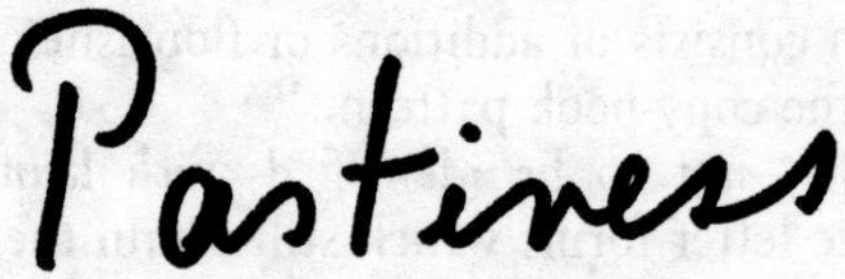

Pastiness

Fig. 34. Pastiness

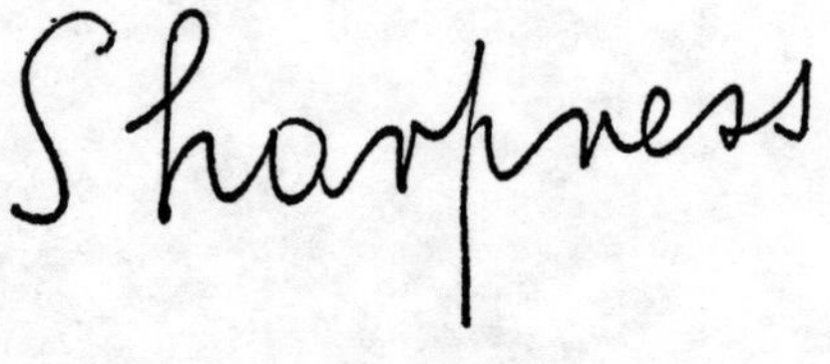

Sharpness

Fig. 35. Sharpness

18 Pastiness and Sharpness

Pastiness in a script symbolises materiality.

It is produced by holding the writing instrument at an angle of considerably less than 90 degrees. Thus the writing is produced by the flat of the instrument as opposed to its point. Pasty strokes are never less than 1/50 inch and the upstrokes and downstrokes have the same thickness.

Pastiness can be interpreted positively as warmth, naturalness, colour sense, refined sensuality.

Negatively it can be interpreted as sensuousness, crudeness, gross materiality, uncouthness.

Sharpness in a script symbolises abstraction.

It is produced by holding the writing instrument at an angle of nearly 90 degrees. Thus the writing is produced by the point of the instrument as opposed to the flat part. Sharp strokes are never more than 1/50 inch and the upstrokes and downstrokes have different thicknesses.

Sharpness can be interpreted positively an analytical-mindedness, spirituality, tenacity, vitality.

Negatively it can be interpreted as quarrelsomeness, resentment, criticism, coldness.

Fig. 36.   Fullness in the upper zone

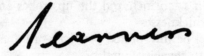

Fig. 37.   Fullness in the middle zone

Fig. 38.   Fullness in the lower zone

Fig. 39.   Leanness in the upper zone

Fig. 40.   Leanness in the middle zone

Fig. 41.   Leanness in the lower zone

19 Fullness and Leanness

A full script is one in which the letters—mainly the looped letters—are larger than the copy-book pattern.

A lean script is one in which the letters—again mainly the looped letters—are smaller than the copy-book pattern.

Fullness in the upper zone can be interpreted positively as vision, imagination, colourful speech, apperception.

Negatively it can be interpreted as day-dreaming, bombast, lack of self-criticism, utopianism.

Fullness in the middle zone can be interpreted positively as sociability, emotionality, heartiness, warm nature.

Negatively it can be interpreted as social climbing, conventionality, compulsive hospitality, amiability.

Fullness in the lower zone can be interpreted positively as erotic fantasies and behaviour, sensuousness, materiality, countryside interests.

Negatively it can be interpreted as perverse fantasies and behaviour, sensuality, earthiness, gross materiality.

Leanness in the upper zone can be interpreted positively as ethical tendencies, rational thinking, analytical mindedness, mental clarity.

Negatively it can be interpreted as irritability, criticism, lack of ideas, lack of imagination.

Leanness in the middle zone can be interpreted positively as matter-of-factness, emotional control, social discrimination, coolness.

Negatively it can be interpreted as rigidity, snobbishness, lack of inner resources, coldness.

Leanness in the lower zone can be interpreted positively as religious and ethical observances, sexual sublimation, business-mindedness, realism.

Negatively it can be interpreted as pessimism, sexual repression, neurotic conscience, money mania.

Fig. 42.   Left and right in the upper zone

Fig. 43.   Left and right in the middle zone

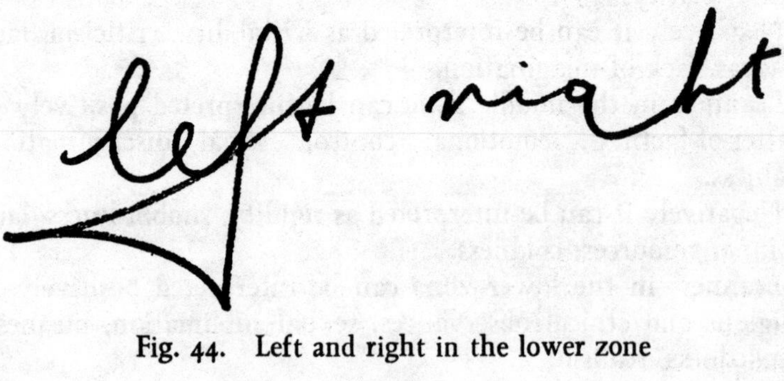

Fig. 44.   Left and right in the lower zone

20 Left and Right Tendencies in the Zones

Left tending movements are seen in those strokes which, according to the copy-book pattern, should be written with a right tending movement. These right tending movements are either omitted or are written with left tending movements. Normal left-tending movements are exaggerated.

Right tending movements are seen in those strokes which, according to the copy-book pattern, should be written with a left tending movement. These left tending movements are either omitted or are written with right tending movements. Normal right-tending movements are exaggerated.

Left tendencies symbolise control, inhibition, egocentricity, introversion.

Right tendencies symbolise relaxation, spontaneity, sociality, extroversion.

Left and right tendencies may be found in one or two or all three zones of a script. *But it is the predominance of a particular movement which has to be determined.*

Left tending movements in the upper zone can be interpreted positively as meditativeness, intellectual and moral freedom, personal recollection, reflexiveness.

Negatively they can be interpreted as egoism, speculation, resentment, pseudo-intellectuality.

Left tending movements in the middle zone can be interpreted positively as self-confidence, self-reliance, self-preservation, independence.

Negatively they can be interpreted as deceit, deviousness, egoism, insincerity.

77

Left tending movements in the lower zone can be interpreted positively as mystical impressionability, motherly instincts, instinctual perception of the past, passive sympathy.

Negatively they can be interpreted as sexual inversion, narcissism, drug addiction, paranoid tendencies.

Right tending movements in the upper zone can be interpreted positively as empathy, impressionability, rapid thinking, rationality.

Negatively they can be interpreted as jumping-to-conclusions, suggestibility, superficial thinking, forgetfulness.

Right tending movements in the middle zone can be interpreted positively as altruism, active sympathy, helpfulness, enterprise.

Negatively they can be interpreted as utopianism, unrestrained sentiment, undiscriminating sociability, restlessness.

Right tending movements in the lower zone can be interpreted positively as dexterity, instinctual understanding, concentration, realistic progress.

Negatively they can be interpreted as cleverness, avoidance of too close contact, materialistic exploitation.

21 Margins

Width of margins varies according to the customs of the particular country. In Germany, for example, scripts tend to have a wide left margin. By contrast, American scripts often omit the left margin. However, the following points are valid for British scripts:

(a) the left margin symbolises the past and the ego
(b) the right margin symbolises the future and society
(c) wide margins symbolise reserve or caution
(d) narrow margins symbolise informality or spontaneity
(e) four equal margins symbolise good taste or mannerism
(f) four missing margins symbolise broad-mindedness or vulgarity.

William Smith

Fig. 45.   An elaborate signature

Bill Smith

Fig. 46.   A straightforward signature

22 Signatures

More than any other part of a script, *the signature symbolises the writer's ego.* Yet the signature alone can never be the sole source for a reliable analysis. Its value lies in a comparison between it and the main body of the script.

If the script and the signature are in agreement, this indicates that the writer behaves in private as he does in public. Discrepancies between signature and text indicate discrepancies between public and private conduct. *But differences due to illegibility must be analysed with extreme care.* Most signatures are illegible to a lesser or greater extent—especially those of professional people who are called upon to sign their names many times in the course of a single day. But illegibility of signature *and text* should warn of duplicity in the writer.

Divergencies between signature and text as regards the size of the writing are more revealing. The signature may be unusually small while the text is large or vice versa. Divergencies in either case indicate that the writer's role in social life is not a genuine expression of his character and personality.

A small signature with an otherwise larger text symbolises an under-rating of the writer's ego in relation to society.

A larger signature with an otherwise smaller script symbolises an over-rating of the writer's ego in relation to society.

These remarks concerning divergencies of *size* apply equally to ornamentation/simplification, heavy/light pressure, pastiness/sharpness, under/over-lining, etc.

But genuine personality—as opposed to pseudo-personality—will also be symbolised by a moderate divergence of size between a smaller text and a larger signature. An overall positive interpretation of the text and signature will determine such genuine personality and individuality.

Differences of size, width, angle, slant, pressure, etc., between

81

the Christian name and the family name (and the corresponding initials) symbolise the relationships between the writer and his family.

Additional flourishes should be interpreted in terms of left and right tending movements in the different zones. And underlinings, etc., emphasise the importance of the writer's ego.

23 Envelope Addresses

If we divide an envelope vertically into two halves and again horizontally into two halves, we then have four quarters:

(a) top left
(b) top right
(c) bottom left
(d) bottom right.

It is against the background of these four divisions that we can interpret the handwriting of the name and address.

A name and address which are placed mainly in *the top left* quarter indicate that the writer is concerned to express himself mainly in the upper zone and with left tending movements.

This can be interpreted positively as reserve in social contacts, caution concerning the future, a respect for the past.

Negatively it can be interpreted as difficulties in establishing social contacts, a distrust in the future, a hampering traditionalism.

A name and address which are placed mainly in *the top right quarter* indicate that the writer is concerned to express himself mainly in the upper zone and with right tending movements.

This can be interpreted positively as empathy, impressionability, rapid thinking.

Negatively it can be interpreted as jumping-to-conclusions, suggestibility, superficial thinking.

A name and address which are placed mainly in *the bottom left quarter* indicate that the writer is concerned to express himself mainly in the lower zone and with left tending movements.

This can be interpreted positively as mystical impressionability, motherly instincts, passive sympathy.

Negatively it can be interpreted as erotic preoccupation,

83

extreme subjectivity, paranoid fears.

A name and address which are placed mainly in *the bottom right quarter* indicate that the writer is concerned to express himself mainly in the lower zone and with right tending movements.

This can be interpreted positively as dexterity, instinctual understanding, realistic progress.

Negatively it can be interpreted as cleverness, avoidance of too close contact, materialistic exploitation.

A name and address which are *placed centrally* can be interpreted positively as mental balance or negatively as a sense of impending catastrophe.

NOTES

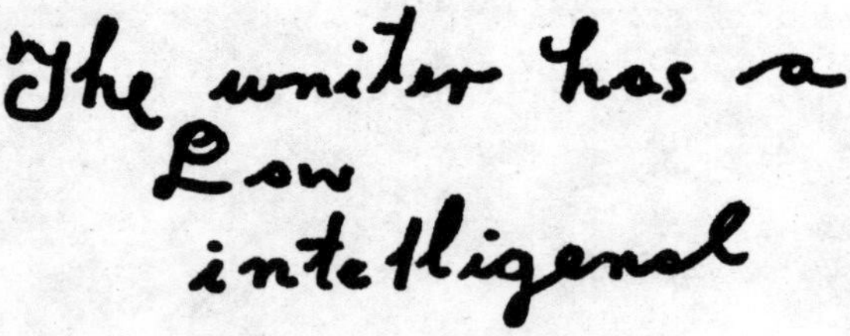

The writer has a Low intelligence

Fig. 47. Low intelligence

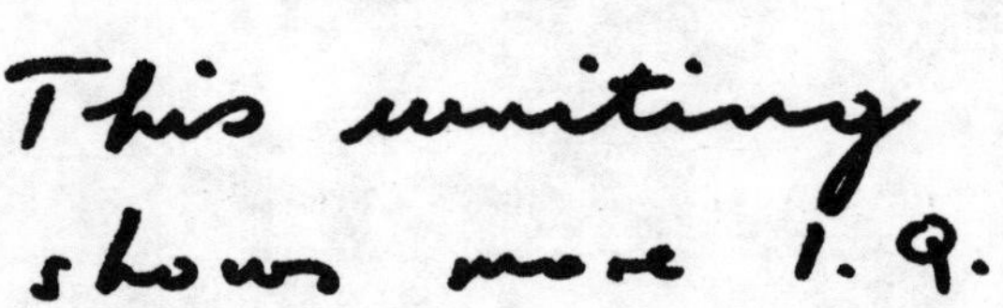

This writing shows more I. Q.

Fig. 48. High intelligence

24 Intelligence

Intelligence means insight and intelligent behaviour is behaviour based on insight into a total situation as opposed to trial-and-error behaviour based on perceptions of mere parts of a situation. Hence intelligent behaviour is an overall pattern composed of many parts. The constituents of this pattern are *memory (the basis of organised mind)*, reason, will, intuition, imagination, invention, creation, assimilation, co-ordination, etc. It has been repeatedly stressed that *a characteral trait is not expressed by any one graphological sign* and in assessing intelligence this is especially true. Rather must many signs be taken into consideration to determine the level of intelligence and the following must be kept in mind:

(a) *originality*
(b) naturalness (but not necessarily)
(c) *good distribution of spaces*
(d) speed (but not of necessity)
(e) *balance and proportion between the zones*
(f) *clever joining-up of 'i' -dots and 't' -bars with the succeeding letters*
(g) simplification (but not necessary)
(h) fluency (but not necessary)
(i) curves (but not necessary)
(j) smallness (but not necessary)

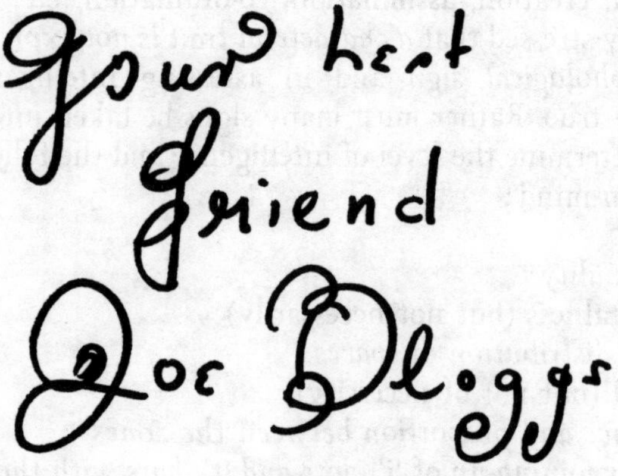

Fig. 49.   Dishonesty in script

25 *Unreliability and Dishonesty*

Like intelligence, unreliability or dishonesty is not a single characteristic. Unreliable or dishonest behaviour is an overall pattern composed of many parts. The constituents of this pattern are selfishness (the chief constituent), materiality, deceit, laziness, indecision, lack of convictions, etc. And of course *unreliability or dishonesty is not expressed by any one graphological sign.* Many signs have to be taken into consideration to determine the level of reliability or unreliability, of honesty or dishonesty and amongst these the following must be kept in mind:

(a) artificiality and stylishness
(b) exaggerations of all kinds (especially in pressure, loops, capitals, signature)
(c) enrollments (especially in initial and terminal strokes)
(d) marked difference between script and signature
(e) mixed writing systems *in an artificial script*
(f) ambiguity in letter execution
(g) covering strokes
(h) illegibility and a leftward slant
(i) writing of wrong letters and words (*especially with an experienced writer*)
(j) broken letters with missing parts
(k) unnecessary re-touching of script in a vain attempt to improve legibility
(l) frequent starts of the initial strokes
(m) missing letters
(n) slowness
(o) impeded flow
(p) arcades (and sometimes threads)
(q) left tendencies, especially in initial and terminal strokes
(r) middle zone loops open at the base

(s) double loops in the middle zone
(t) lack of originality
(u) poor distribution of spaces
(v) 'a', 'd', 'g' and similar letters are written in two separate strokes
(w) extreme enrollments embodied in letter 'I'
(x) weak 't' -bars
(y) extreme activity or passivity
(z) ink-filled loops in the lower zone
   etc.

(SEE PAGE 95, CHAPTER 26)

Fig. 50. Plain capital 'I'

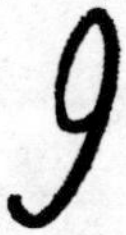
Fig. 51. Capital 'I' with enrollment in the upper zone

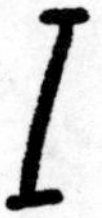
Fig. 52. Capital 'I' in printed form

Fig. 53. Small 'i' without dot

Fig. 54. Small 'i' with dot placed high

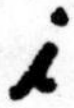
Fig. 55. Small 'i' with dot placed low

(SEE PAGE 95, CHAPTER 26)

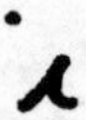
Fig. 56. Small 'i' with dot placed to left

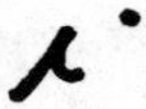
Fig. 57. Small 'i' with dot placed to right

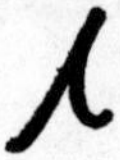
Fig. 58. Small 't' with bar missing

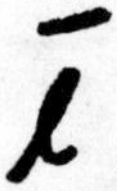
Fig. 59. Small 't' with bar placed high

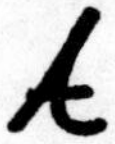
Fig. 60. Small 't' with bar placed low

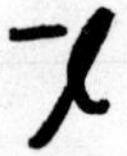
Fig. 61. Small 't' with bar placed left

(SEE PAGE 95, CHAPTER 26)

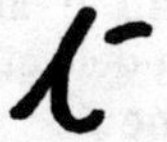

Fig. 62. Small 't' with bar placed right

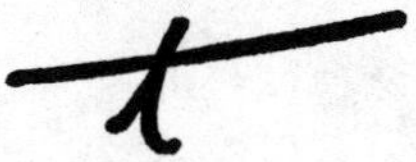

Fig. 63. Small 't' with bar going forcefully through stem

Fig. 64. Small 'a' with long initial stroke

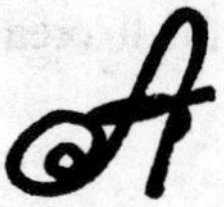

Fig. 65. Capital 'A' with initial enrollment

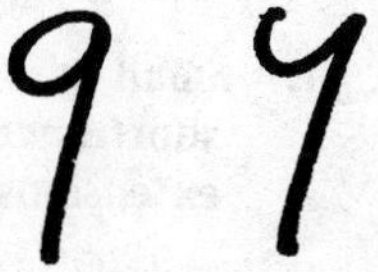

Fig. 66. Small 'g' and 'y' with incomplete lower zone

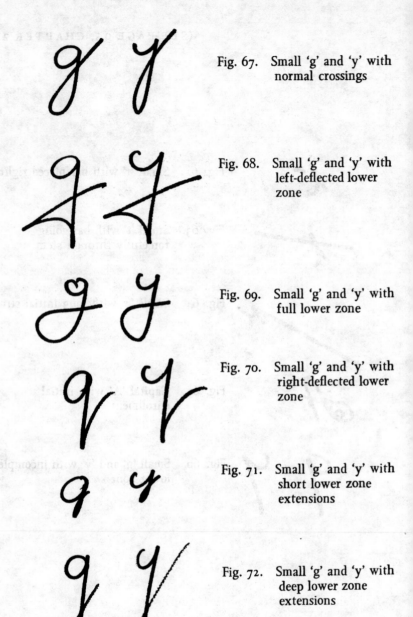

Fig. 67.   Small 'g' and 'y' with normal crossings

Fig. 68.   Small 'g' and 'y' with left-deflected lower zone

Fig. 69.   Small 'g' and 'y' with full lower zone

Fig. 70.   Small 'g' and 'y' with right-deflected lower zone

Fig. 71.   Small 'g' and 'y' with short lower zone extensions

Fig. 72.   Small 'g' and 'y' with deep lower zone extensions

26 Miscellaneous: The Letters 'I' and 'T'; Initial and Terminal Letters; Loops in the Lower Zone

The fact that a number of graphological items are here listed under a section entitled 'Miscellaneous' suggests in no way that they are of minor importance. On the contrary, *everything in graphology is of equal and major importance.* They are arranged thus merely for ease of presentation.

The capital letter 'I' (and its small form 'i') symbolises our attitudes concerning our egos. But conclusions concerning the writer's ego cannot be based on a study of this letter only—a careful study of the signature, of initials, of initial letters of the middle zone must all be taken into consideration. Here we must confine ourselves to a few points out of many.

(a) a plain 'I' can be interpreted positively as essentiality or negatively as dullness (Fig. 50)
(b) a printed 'I' can be interpreted positively as cultural interests or negatively as mannerism (Fig. 52)
(c) a capital 'I' with enrollments in the upper and/or lower zone(s) can be interpreted positively as shrewdness or negatively as opportunism (Fig. 51)
(d) a small 'i' without the dot can be interpreted only negatively: carelessness, irresponsibility, unreliability (Fig. 53)
(e) 'i'-dots should be interpreted according to position (high/medium/low, left/centre/right), pressure, shape (round/accent), etc. (Figs. 54-57)
   T-bars, especially of the small 't's, should also be interpreted

95

according to position (high/medium/low/missing, left/centre/right), pressure, direction (rising/horizontal/falling), shape (concave, convex), etc. (Figs. 58-63).

Initial strokes which are long indicate the pull of the past Broken initial strokes (indicating repeated attempts to start) symbolise obsessions and self-doubts. Enrollments on initial strokes symbolise shrewdness or opportunism (Figs. 64, 65).

Terminal strokes which end abruptly symbolise abruptness or ruthlessness. Extended terminal strokes symbolise sociality or matiness if in the middle zone; abstraction or unrealism if the termination is in the upper zone; communal pleasures of an instinctual kind if the termination is in the lower zone. These interpretations concerning terminal strokes are valid *only when the stroke is gentle and curved*. If the stroke is straight or angular, sharp or blunt, then the interpretations would be based accordingly on such factors as coldness, hardness, aggressiveness or brutality.

Lower zone loops, such as are found in 'f', 'g', 'j', 'y', 'z', are of significance *within the total evaluation of the script* (Figs. 66-72).

It is the flexor muscles which enable such lower zone movements to be carried out. Flexor movements are associated with primary pleasures such as sexual activities, eating, drinking, erotic pleasures involving the skin and bodily movements—cutaneous and muscular eroticism respectively. So the deeper the downstroke extends in the vertical plane and the more it extends left after it has reached its maximum descent, the more is the libido cathected on to objects in the material sphere of personality. But the shorter the downstroke and the shorter the left turning movement after the maximum descent has been reached, the less is the libido cathected on to objects in the material sphere of personality. Sometimes the loop is deep, wide, full (and therefore complete). This can be interpreted as, among other possibilities, a strong sexual imagination. Sometimes there is no loop at all, merely a downstroke. Among possible interpretations, this can symbolise sublimation, essentiality, fatalism. Sometimes the loop is narrow and pointed. This may symbolise, among other possibilities, criticism. Sometimes the downstroke

96

is broken. There are many possible interpretations for this: neglect, fatigue, dishonesty, etc. The point is that *lower zone loops have to be evaluated according to many factors*: pressure, fullness/leanness, sharpness/pastiness, etc., etc.

27 Graphology and Depth Psychology

A systematic study of graphology cannot ignore the concepts, techniques or findings of depth psychology. There are today many schools of depth psychology but we shall confine our attention to the schools of Freud (the father of depth psychology), Jung and Szondi.

Freud assumes that mental life is the function of an apparatus to which he ascribes the characteristics of being extended in space and of being made up of several portions. The bodily organ of the psyche is the brain and nervous system.

The oldest portion or agency of the mind is the 'id' which is the inherited reservoir of the instincts which latter are the mental presentation of somatic demands.

There are two basic groups of instincts: Eros (the life instincts) and Thanatos (the death instincts). Freud designated the energy of Eros as 'libido'. The energy of Thanatos has been designated, by Schilder, as 'mortido'—it is sometimes referred to as 'destrudo'.

The id functions according to the 'pleasure principle' which requires that instinctual tensions be lowered immediately.

The 'ego' is that portion or agency of the mind which was developed out of the cortical layer of the id. It functions according to the 'reality principle' because it was adapted for receiving and excluding stimuli. Hence its relationship to reality is of first importance.

The 'super-ego' is derived from four main sources:

(a) the 'ego-ideal' (formed in imagination to compensate for the deficiencies of the 'real-ego')
(b) 'introjection' (the phantasying of images of lost objects)
(c) 'nemessism' (aggression turned against the subject)

98

(d) 'sado-masochism' (outwardly and inwardly directed aggression involving both pleasant and painful stimuli).

The super-ego is the ethico-moral agency of the mind.

The concepts of id, ego, super-ego constitute the Freudian mental topography. The theory of the instincts constitutes the mental dynamics. The concepts of the 'mental mechanisms' (the distributors of mental energy) constitute the mental economics.

The bases of Freudian psychoanalysis are:

(a) infantile sexuality
(b) repression
(c) conflict
(d) the unconscious
(e) transference.

The sexual life is di-phasic: the first efflorescence is separated from the second efflorescence by the 'latency period'. The first efflorescence culminates for the boy in the 'Oedipus complex' and for the girl in the 'Elektra complex'. The sexual development proceeds in these overlapping stages:

(a) oral (the mouth is the main focus of interest with the corresponding activities of sucking, eating, drinking, etc)
(b) anal (the anus is the main focus of interest with the corresponding activities of defecating, passing flatus, etc)
(c) urethral (the urethra and penis are the main foci of interest with the corresponding activities of urinating, bed-wetting, etc)
(d) phallic (the penis is the main focus of interest culminating in the Oedipus complex and the latency period and accompanied by the corresponding activities of penal manipulation)
(e) genital (the penis once more—with the end of the latency period—is the main focus of interest with the corresponding activities of genital sexuality).

Repression is the consequence of super-ego censorship.

99

Conflict is the inevitable consequence of such repression.

Repression and conflict necessitate the further concept of the unconscious.

Transference is the displacement on to a substitute object (a parent-figure substitute) of a subject's infantile feelings, ideas, etc.

Dreams are temporary psychoses during the sleeping state. Consequently, the function of reality-testing, applied to experiences in both the inner and outer world, is inhibited. Errors of perception arise and these are called hallucinations. Two mental mechanisms prominent in dream-activity are 'condensation' (the process by which two or more images combine or can be combined to form a composite image which is invested with meaning and energy derived from both) and 'displacement' (the process by which mental energy is transferred from one mental image to another). The dream, as experienced by the dreamer, is the manifest dream but the real dream-process is expressed in the latent dream. The origin of the dream is either an experience of the immediate past, now in the 'pre-conscious' (ideas, feelings, etc which are descriptively unconscious but not repressed) or an instinctual demand from the id. These are the 'ontogenetic' (individual developmental) aspects of the dream. Dreams with archaic content express the 'phylogenetic' aspects (aspects relating to the development of the species) of the id. But the essential function of dream-work is wish-fulfilment through compromise.

Freudian psychoanalytical technique is an investigational procedure for the understanding and explaining of the unconscious. It interprets the 'primary processes' of mind, that is to say, those mental processes existing before the structured ego and before the development of verbalisation. While it certainly does not ignore the phylogenetic aspects of mind, it is primarily concerned with mind in its ontogenetic aspects (see page 39).

In *Analytical Psychology*, Jung defines the psyche as 'the totality of all psychological processes, both conscious as well as unconscious'. The conscious and the unconscious are opposed in their properties but they complement each other. The unconscious is older than the conscious and the former is the fundamental functioning upon which the latter is built. The unconscious has two aspects : the personal and the collective. The personal unconscious consists of personal repressions, the collective unconscious of both primitive drives and archaic content possessed of elemental force.

Within the psyche there are four functions : thinking, feeling, intuition, sensation. They are complementary or compensatory.

Extroversion and introversion are the two general psychological attitudes which determine the manner in which a person will react to different situations.

Jung says of the collective unconscious that it is '. . . the might spiritual inheritance of human development, reborn in every individual . . . constitution'. The first conscious manifestations of the unconscious are symptoms and complexes. Symptoms can be defined as phenomena of obstruction of the normal flow of energy and they can manifest themselves physically or psychically. Complexes are 'psychological parts split off from the personality'.

Dreams, fantasies and visions are all manifestations of the unconscious. They are not bound by time, space or casuality and they are regulating activities of the unconscious—thus preventing one-sidedness.

The total psychic functioning is in unceasing dynamic movement. 'Libido' is the theoretical postulate for the psychic energy, the unceasing movement of which is caused by a difference of potential, as expressed by one of the pair of opposites. Because of the 'law of complementariness', energy will flow from an unconscious, undifferentiated attitude or function to a conscious, over-differentiated attitude or function. Thus the Jungian psyche is a self-regulating system and, says Jung, 'there is no equibrium and no self-regulating system without opposition'.

The libido is directed either forward by the conscious or backward by the unconscious. It can also be 'transformed' from one of a pair of opposites to the other by an act of will.

The 'image' is the specific form of manifestation of energy in the psyche. It possesses a 'value-intensity' as measured by its 'constellation' and there can be no set symbols—this applies also in dream-analysis.

In dealing with the psyche one is dealing with intangibles

which exhibit apparent contradiction and are governed by 'either and/or'. It is a dialectic process of thesis, anthesis and 'tertium quid'.

The contents of the collective unconscious manifest themselves with the appearance of 'archetypes'—the psychic counterparts of 'instincts'. A particular archetype predominates at a particular stage of life. The archetypes are:

(a) 'shadow' (the 'dark side' of our nature)
(b) 'anima' (the contra-sexual in the male)
(c) 'animus' (the contra-sexual in the female)
(d) 'persona' (façade exhibited to society)
(e) 'old wise man' (the spiritual principle in the male)
(f) 'Magna mater' (the great earth-mother)
(g) 'self' (the ending of the polarity by a synthesis)

Jungian Analytical or Complex Psychology understands the phylogenesis of mind in terms of collective archetypal phenomena within an acausalistic and finalistic framework. The ontogenesis of mind it treats as of secondary importance. It is a psychology of the 'secondary processes' (thinking processes which obey the laws of grammar and formal logic, use bound energy and are governed by the Freudian reality-principle) because Jung did not accept the bases of Freudian psychoanalysis: infantile sexuality, repression, conflict, the unconscious, transference. Moreover, Jungian symbol-interpretation is in terms of concrete to abstract whereas Freudian interpretation is from the abstract to the concrete— e.g. 'penis' to a Jungian means 'sexuality' but to a Freudian 'sexuality' means 'penis'.

In Schicksalpsychology (the psychology of fate/destiny), Szondi postulates, in addition the Freudian unconscious and the Jungian collective unconscious, the 'familial unconscious' the contents of which are the psychological tendencies of our ancestors which we inherit. This content is transmitted from one generation to the next by the agency of latent recessive genes and it was to investigate character and personality in terms of genetic activity and influence that Szondi developed his experimental diagnostic test. This consists of forty-eight photographs of psycho-pathological personalities, taken from psychiatric text-books extending back to 1892. There are six photographs of each of the following eight psycho-pathological types:

(a) homosexuals
(b) sadists and murderers
(c) epileptics
(d) hysterics
(e) catatonic schizonphrenics
(f) paranoid schizophrenics
(g) depressed stages of manic-depressives
(h) manic stage of manic-depressives

It is sufficient to say that the testee is asked to express his likes and dislikes concerning each of the forty-eight photographs in turn.

Szondi sees human behaviour as being motivated by eight drive-systems or need-systems which are as follows:

(a) the need to be passive (the 'h' factor)
(b) the need to be active (the 's' factor) } the 'h' and 's' factors constitute the sexual vector

(c) the need to experience strong feel-ings (the 'e' factor)
(d) the need to experience fine feelings (the 'hy' factor) } the 'e' and 'hy' factors constitute the paroxysmal vector

(e) the need to withdraw from the environment (the 'k' factor)
(f) the need to fuse with the environ-ment (the 'p' factor) } the 'k' and 'p' factors constitute the ego vector

(g) the need to seek objects (the 'd' factor)
(h) the need to cling to objects (the 'm' factor) } the 'd' and 'm' factors constitute the contact vector

The manifestation of the *extreme* form of each of these drives or needs corresponds with the behaviour of each of the eight psycho-pathological types. In human behaviour, there is no absolute normal or absolute abnormal—the normal gradually merges into the abnormal.

Each of these drives or needs can be accepted or denied. Each of the vectors is polar and in health the eight needs are balanced but in mental or characteral disorders they become unbalanced. For example, 'k' needs (inherited or acquired) can be socialised or humanised in work requiring logic or systematisation but unsatisfied 'k' needs can result in catatonic schizophrenia.

Szondi accepts the Freudian pleasure principle and reality principle. Additionally he postulates the 'humanitarian principle'. *This means that every drive has both psychopathological as well as humanised possibilities.* The psychopathological possibilities constitute the compulsive destiny/fate —the humanised possibilities constitute the volitional destiny/ fate. And the deciding factor is the freedom of the Spirit.

The foregoing outline sketches of the Freudian, Jungian and Szondian depth psychologies have been given because I believe that if graphology ignores the findings of depth psychology it is cutting itself off from a most fertile source of knowledge concerning human motivation and human behaviour. *And there are still far too many graphologists at the present time who are mere dabblers in depth psychology.*

The graphological features corresponding to orality and the Szondian 'm' factor are:
(a) ovals open at the top (a's and o's)
(b) fullness in the lower zone
(c) large terminal letters
(d) poor distribution of spaces
(e) lack of originality
(f) garlands or arcades
(g) right slant
(h) uneven pressure

The graphological features symbolising anality and the Szondian 'd' factor are:
(a) pastiness
(b) fullness in the lower zone
(c) large terminal letters
(d) abrupt terminal strokes

(e) ink-filled lower zone loops
(f) narrow script
(g) upright or left slanting script
(h) angular connections
(i) heavy pressure
(j) artificiality
(k) lack of originality
(l) 'i'-dots and 't'-bars pointed or blunted
(m) poor distribution of spaces

It will be noted that there are certain graphological features common to both the oral type and the anal type. This must be so because *orality and anality are two aspects of pre-genital sexuality*, that is to say, of sexual immaturity.

The graphological features symbolising passivity, receptivity and the Szondian 'h' factor are:
(a) light pressure
(b) atypical forms of lower zone loops
(c) the use of green or light blue inks
(d) left slanting script
(e) low-placed or missing 'i'-dots and 't'-bars
(f) fullness in the lower zone
(g) thready connection or garlands
(h) slow script
(i) rather pasty
(j) ornamentation
(k) wide script with light pressure
(l) irregular script

The graphological features symbolising activity, impressiveness and the Szondian 's' factor are:
(a) angular connections
(b) high pressure
(c) large size
(d) right slant
(e) speed
(f) firm downstrokes

(g) 't'-bars downwards, pointed, high-placed, long, heavy
(h) large capitals
(i) open ovals
(j) heavy terminal strokes

The graphological features symbolising violent emotions and the Szondian factor 'e' are:
(a) heavy 't'-bars and terminal strokes
(b) angular connections
(c) uneven pressure
(d) broken letters
(e) ink blots
(f) variable height of letters (especially in middle zone)
(g) irregular base line
(h) bad spacing between lines
(i) unusual formations in the lower zone

The graphological features symbolising fine feelings and the Szondian factor 'hy' are:
(a) thready and/ or garland connections
(b) irregularity
(c) exaggerations of all kinds
(d) fullness and ornamentations
(e) broken letters and/or neglected letters
(f) over-connected or disconnected script
(g) excessive left or right tendencies
(h) uneven base line
(i) much underlining and excessive punctuation

The graphological features symbolising ego-contraction, ego-withdrawal, the Szondian 'k' factor are:
(a) horizontal straight lines
(b) carefully placed 't'-bars and 'i'-dots
(c) good distribution of spaces
(d) simplification
(e) regularity
(f) smallness
(g) upright script

(h) printed capital 'I'
(i) connected script
(j) sharpness
(k) slowness
(l) legibility
(m) even pressure
(n) leanness in the upper zone
(o) naturalness
(p) originality
(q) narrow script with pressure

The graphological features symbolising ego-expansion, ego-participation, the Szondian 'p' factor are:
(a) straight or rising lines
(b) high-placed 't'-bars and 'i'-dots
(c) ornamentation
(d) large script
(e) large and elaborated capital 'I'
(f) large and elaborated signature
(g) heavy pressure
(h) arcade connections
(i) large capitals
(j) extensions into upper and lower zones
(k) exaggerated right tending 't'-bars
(l) sham originality
(m) artificiality
(n) ambiguity
(o) mixed writing systems
(p) enrollments
(q) thready connections
(r) much underlining (especially of signature)
(s) wide upper margin
(t) 'd' and 'o' open at the base

It is not claimed that the graphological features relating to each of the above eight types are all the possible features for each type—after all we are dealing with mind (Geist) not nature. Again it must be remarked that graphological features are

107

common to more than one of the eight types because the 'h' and the 's' are polar opposites, as are the 'e' and 'hy', the 'k' and 'p', the 'd' and 'm'. Moreover the 'h', 'hy', 'p', 'm' are all related to each other, as are also the 's', 'e', 'k', 'd' to each other.

But in spite of the highly significant insights provided by the schools of depth psychology into character and personality, there are very real difficulties encountered when attempts are made to study depth psychological types within terms of graphological features. This is because a depth psychological technique (in particular, the Szondi test) aims *directly* at the unconscious sphere of psychic events. This is in contrast with handwriting-analysis which first analyses the subject's behaviour phenomenologically (as revealed in his handwriting) and only by this method attempts to uncover the manifestations of unconscious drives.

Methodologically, the two techniques may be considered thus:

(a) the Szondi test (as a method of natural science) investigates directly the unconscious ego and drives; thus the feelings and emotions; thus the behaviour (erotic, occupational and social)

(b) graphological-analysis (as a method of Geisteswissenschaft) provides a phenomenological insight into feelings, emotions, intelligence, will, conduct; and thus into the conscious ego; and thus into the unconscious ego and drives.

28 Trait Index

Accuracy: exact placing of 'i'-dots and 't'-bars; good spacing.

Activity: angles; high pressure; large size; rightward-slant; firm downstroke; speedy.

Adaptability: garlands; curved forms; moderate speed; even pressure.

Adventurousness: over-sized upper and lower zones but normal sized middle zone; originality; naturalness; good spacing.

Aesthetic sense: printed letter (especially capitals); good distribution of spaces.

Aggressiveness: angles; speed; heavy pressure.

Agility: low pressure in combination with a regular script; speed.

Altruism: right-tending movements in the middle zone.

Ambition: uneven pressure; speed; large capitals; rising 't' bars; rising lines; extensions into upper and lower zones.

Amiability: fluency; low 't'-bars; right slope; garlands.

Analytical-mindedness: sharp script; good spacing; simplification.

Anger: 't'-bars and terminal strokes heavy; high and pointed

Ascetism: sharp script; simplified script.

Apprehensiveness: up strokes broken in the upper zone; variable height of middle zone.

Assertiveness: large capitals; open ovals; high-placed 't'-bars downwards or pointed.

Authority: exaggerated right-tending 't'-bars.

Balance: naturalness; originality; good distribution of spaces.

Benevolence: garlands.

Broad-mindedness: small size; garlands; upright script.

Brutality: terminal strokes broadening; heavy pressure; irregularity.

Calmness: 'i'-dots and 't'-bars placed low; curves; slowness; even pressure.

Carefulness: exact placing of 'i'-dots and 't'-bars; legibility; regular spacing; even pressure; slowness.

Carelessness: misplaced or omitted 'i'-dots or 't'-bars; illegibility; irregular spacing; uneven pressure; speed.

Caution: 'i'-dots and 't'-bars light and/or precise; initial adjustments; closed ovals.

Chattiness: narrow spacing; uneven script with entanglement between the lines; a's and o's open at top.

Ceremoniousness: large capitals; flourishes; sham originality; artificiality.

Chivalry: large script; fullness; ornamentation.

Clarity: simplification of script; leanness in the upper zone; good distribution of spacing; naturalness; originality.

Coarseness: ungraceful forms; ink blots; heavy pressure.

Coldness: sharpness; backward-slant.

Colourfulness: ornamentation; fullness; large capitals; heavy pressure; originality.

Conceit: artificiality; large capitals; flourishes (especially in signature).

Concentration: 'i'-dots and 't'-bars placed low; small script; vertical.

109

TRAIT INDEX

Confidence: garlands; rightward-slant; rising lines; rising 't'-bars.

Conscientiousness: low-placed 'i'-dots and 't'-bars; legibility; sharpness.

Constancy: regular script; angles.

Constructiveness: use of concave; printed letters; originality.

Contemplativeness: undersized upper and lower zones but normal middle zone; regular script.

Coolness: leanness (especially in the middle zone); a narrow script with pressure.

Courage: heavy pressure (especially with terminal strokes); good distribution of spaces.

Criticism: sharp script in its negative interpretation; leanness in the upper zone; narrow script with pressure.

Cruelty: 'i'-dots and 't'-bars heavy and pointed; terminals pointed and downward; pasty; heavy pressure.

Culture: good spacing, naturalness; originality; printed letters.

Cunning: ambiguity; mixed writing systems with artificiality; upright or left-slant; artificiality; slowness.

Curiosity: high-placed 'i'-dots and 't'-bars; letters of middle zone pointed at top.

Deceit: 'd' and 'o' open at base; ambiguity; irregular base line.

Depression: terminal stroke of last letter extended weakly into lower zone; descending line.

Determination: angles; abrupt endings to terminal strokes and 't'-bars with heavy pressure; general heavy pressure.

Devotion: ascending lines; exaggerated right-tending 't'-bars; right-slant; small size.

Dexterity: right-tending movements in the lower zone; thready connection; right-slant.

Diplomacy: terminal letter diminishing; artificiality; upright script; closed ovals.

Directness: omission of initial strokes; simplification.

Discussion: sharp script in its positive interpretation.

Dishonesty: see pages 89, 90.

Dominativeness: regular script; large capitals; long and heavy 't'-bars.

Dreaminess: low pressure; fullness in the upper zone; ornamentation; high-placed i's and t's.

Eccentricity: unusual punctuation; ornamentation; artificiality; highly individualised script.

Economy: narrow script with pressure; narrow spacing; slowness.

Egoism: very full capital 'I's; enrollments to left; large capitals; flourishings and underlinings (especially in signature).

Elasticity: low pressure in combination with a regular script; thready connection; irregular script.

Elation: rising lines and 't'-bars; high-placed and right-tending 'i'-dots.

Enduringness: high pressure in combination with a regular script.

Energy: heavy pressure; firm down strokes; angles.

Enjoyment: pasty script; straight or rising lines.

Ennui: low pressure in irregular script; descending 't'-bars and 'i'-dots; slow; descending lines.

Enterprise: right-tending movements in the middle zone; over-sized upper and lower zone but normal middle zone; large script.

Enthusiasm: ascending 't'-bars which are long and high-placed; ascending lines; rather speedy; rather heavy pressure.

Eroticism: fullness in the lower zone in its negative interpretation; left-tending movements in the lower zone with pressure; ink-filled loops.

Ethical behaviour: leanness in the upper zone; small script; sharpness.

Exaggeration: large script; large capitals; flourishes; high-placed 'i'-dots and 't'-bars; inflated extensions into the upper and lower zones.

Excitability: high-placed 'i'-dots and 't'-bars in the form of dashes; irregular script; thready connection; rising lines.

Extravagance: wide margins or widening margins (especially in Britain); wide spacing; large writing.

Family pride: family initial written large throughout script; family name written larger than first name; family name written larger than main body of script.

Far-sightedness: large script in combination with regularity; over-sized upper and lower zones but normal middle zone.

Fatigue: descending lines; irregular script; weak pressure.

Fearfulness: low pressure; narrow spacing; upstrokes broken in the upper zone.

Femininity: low pressure in combination with a regular script.

Firmness: angles, regular script; strong 't'-bars.

Flexibility: thready connection; upright script.

Formality: wide upper margin; ornamentation; wide spacing.

Frankness: wide script with pressure; garlands.

Friendliness: naturalness; garlands; right slant; right extension.

Generosity: wide spacing of words; right extension of terminal strokes.

Gentleness: curves (especially garlands); medium to light pressure.

Hardness: negative interpretation of angular script; sharpness.

Heartiness: fullness in the middle zone; pastiness.

Hesitancy: slow script in its negative interpretation.

Honesty: see pages 89, 90.

Hospitality: all four margins missing; garlands; terminal strokes extended to the right.

Humility: small script; simplification (especially of capital 'I').

Humour: wavy horizontal strokes.

Hypersensitivity: wide script with light pressure; irregular script with low pressure; left tendencies relating to capital 'I'.

Hypocrisy: arcade formations in letters; irregular base line; 'd' and 'o' open at the base.

Idealism: low pressure in combination with an irregular script; large size in combination with an irregular script; predominance of the upper zone.

Imagination: high-placed 'i'-dots and 't'-bars; emphasis on the upper zone.

Impartiality: small size in combination with an irregular script; vertical.

Impatience: 'i'-dots and 't'-bars placed to the right; angles; right slant; negative interpretation of wide script with low pressure; speed.

Imperiousness: large size; flourishes (especially in signature); ornamentation.

Impressionability: wide script with light pressure; irregular script with low pressure.

Inactivity: curves; light pressure; slow.

Independence: large capitals; angles; first strokes of 'M', 'N', 'W' are higher than remaining strokes.

Individualism: disconnected script; upright script; originality; naturalness; good spacing; speed.

Informality: narrow left margin; simplification.

Initiative: right slant; connected or disconnected script; low pressure in combination with a regular script; speed; originality.

Instability: variable speed; 'i'-dots and 't'-bars placed in the form of dashes; high pressure in irregular script.

Intelligence: see page 87.

Intuition: disconnected script.

Inventiveness: disconnected script; simplification; originality; good distribution of spaces; naturalness.

Irresolution: variable pressure and slant; variable placing of 'i'-dots and 't'-bars; rather slow script.

Irritability: variable height of letters; angles; high-placed 'i'-dots and 't'-bars.

Jest: wavy horizontal strokes.

Joy: large script; rising lines; rather heavy pressure.

Judiciousness: upper zone extension with leanness, uprightness and angularity.

Keenness: sharp script in its negative interpretation.

Kindness: all four margins missing; garlands; right slant.

Languidness: weak pressure; descending lines.

Largess: large script; negative interpretation of upper zone predominance.

Lassitude: weak pressure; descending lines.

Leniency: garlands; upright script; all four margins missing.

Lethargy: slow script; negative interpretation of garlands.

Loftiness: extensions and fullness in the upper zone; high-placed 'i'-dots and 't'-bars; script above base line.

Loquaciousness: rising lines; 'o's open at top.

Loyalty: upright or left slant; pastiness.

Lucidity: good organisation of spacing; simplification.

Mannerism: ornamentation; flourishes (especially in signature) negative interpretation of arcade script.

Masculinity: high pressure in combination with a regular script.

Materialism: predominance of the lower zone (especially with ink-filled loops); negative interpretation of pastiness; negative interpretation of leanness in the lower zone.

Maturity: simplification; originality; naturalness; good distribution of spaces.

Methodicalness: horizontal straight lines; carefully placed 't'-bars and 'i'-dots; good distribution of spaces.

Mimicry: negative interpretation of a thready script.

Miserliness: no margins; terminal strokes short or hooked; narrow spacing between words and lines.

Moderateness: narrow script with pressure; undersized upper and lower zone but normal middle zone; regular script.

Modesty: small script; small capitals; naturalness; simplification.

Moodiness: negative interpretation of an irregular script; rising and falling lines; variable pressure.

Naturalness: pastiness; speed; garlands.

Neighbourliness: wide script with pressure; right slant; garlands; connected script; right tendencies in the middle zone.

Nervousness: sudden changes in pressure, speed and size.

Neutrality: upright script.

Observation: first stroke of 'r' is higher than second; letter 'e' is concave shaped; small script; undersized upper and lower zones but normal middle zone; disconnected script.

Obstinacy: terminal strokes accentuated and hooked; heavy pressure; 't'-bars heavy and hooked.

Open-mindedness: garlands; irregularity; upright script.

Optimism: ascending lines and 't'-bars; high-placed 'i'-dots; firm strokes; wide and right slanting script.

Orderliness: even margins; regular script; good distribution of spaces.

Originality: tasteful ornamentation; simplification; legible deviations from the copy-book.

Passion: heavy strokes; pastiness; angles; large script; right slant.

Patience: exactly-placed 'i'-dots and 't'-bars; slowness; curves.

Perception: rather fast; small script; good vertical spacing; placing of 'i'-dots and 't'-bars causes letter connections to be broken.

Perseverance: horizontal straight lines; angles; hooks.

Pessimism: descending lines; weak pressure; weak 'i'-dots and 't'-bars.

Poise: vertical slant; garlands; arcades; regular script.

Possessiveness: left tending enrollments; enrollments of capitals; enrollments of initials.

Practicality: curled extensions in the upper zone; short terminal strokes; exaggerated extensions in the lower zone; curtailed extensions in the upper zone; narrow margins; narrow spacing between words.

Precaution: narrowing left margin; wide right margin; left slant.

Pride: large script; oversized capitals and signature; much underlining; wide left margin; upright script; four exact margins; ornamentation.

Procrastination: 'i'-dots and 't'-bars placed to left of stroke; rather slow.

Progressiveness: right tending movements; absence of left tending movements; right slant; high-placed 'i'-dots and 't'-bars; speed; ascending lines.

Prudence: low-placed and carefully-placed 'i'-dots and 't'-bars; slowness; upright or left slanting script; narrowing left margin; wide right margin.

Quaintness: deviations from the copy-book; ornamentation; much underlining; exaggerations of all kinds (especially of capitals, signature, punctuation).

Querulousness: negative interpretation of sharp script; angular script with pressure; hooks.

Radicalism: negative interpretation of right slant; rising lines; very highly placed 'i'-dots and 't'-bars; absence of left tending movements.

Rationality: upright script; leanness in the upper zone; simplification; straight lines; firm 't'-bars; low-placed 'i'-dots.

Realism: leanness in the lower zone; predominance in the lower zone; small script in combination with regularity.

Reasoning: connected script.

Receptivity: high pressure in combination with an irregular script.

Reproductive Intelligence: connected script; absence of originality (in particular of simplification or of ornamentation).

Reserve: arcades; left tendencies and movements; wide right margin; wide lower margin; upright script; narrow script with pressure.

Resistance: high pressure with regularity; angles; hooks; firm and falling 't'-bars.

Resoluteness: 'i'-dots and 't'-bars placed heavy and firm (accentuated by hooks); rather fast script.

Respectfulness: low-placed 't'-bars; simplification; small script; first stroke of 'M' and 'W' smaller than other strokes.

Restraint: negative interpretation of angular script; positive interpretation of left slant; small script; regularity.

Secretiveness: left tending terminal arcade; arcade connections; left tending enrollments in the upper zone.

Self-discipline: sharpness; small script; regularity; simplification; upright script; firm, even pressure; good distribution of spaces.

Selfishness: very full capital 'I's; enrollments to left; large capitals; flourishings and underlinings (especially in signature); pastiness; large script; ornamentation; left slant (sometimes upright); uneven pressure; bad distribution of spaces; poor form level.

Sensuality: pastiness; ink-filled loops; fullness in the lower zone.

Sensitiveness: extreme right slant; wavering lines; pressure with irregularity.

Seriousness: absence of wavy horizontal strokes; angles; large script; regularity; firm 't'-bars.

Shrewdness: closed ovals; short terminal strokes; enrollments (especially in capitals and initials).

Shyness: wide right margin; thready connection with occasional flourishes (especially in signature); absence of ornamentation; oversized upper and lower zones.

Sincerity: see pages 89, 90.

Sociability: right tending movements in the middle zone; connected script; garlands; right slant; wide script with pressure.

Spirituality: sharpness; light pressure; exaggerated extensions in the upper zone.

Stability: low and firmly-placed 'i'-dots and 't'-bars; steady speed; even pressure with regularity.

Stupidity: see page 87.

Submissiveness: capital 'I' written in the form of small 'i'; low-placed 't'-bars; simplification; small script; first strokes of 'M' and 'W' smaller than other strokes; positive interpretation of left slant; regularity; narrow script.

Superiority: artificiality; ornamentation; large script; heavy pressure; large capitals (especially in initials); signature larger than text; many flourishes and much underlining (especially in signature); oversized capital 'I'; second stroke of 'M' and second and third strokes of 'W' written larger than first stroke.

Sympathy: right tending movements in the middle zone; garlands; right slant; wide script with low pressure.

Tactfulness: closed ovals; terminal letters increasing in size; narrow script; upright or left tendencies.

Tactlessness: open ovals; terminal letters decreasing in size; wide script with pressure; right tendencies.

Taste: deviations and ornamentations from the copy-book which are harmonious and balanced; four exact margins; originality; naturalness; good distribution of spaces.

Tenacity: hooks; angles; sharpness; high pressure with regularity.

Thoughtfulness: upright script; careful execution of 'i'-dots and 't'-bars; sharpness; emphasis in the upper zone; regularity.

Thoughtlessness: extreme left or right slant; careless execution of 'i'-dots and 't'-bars; ambiguity of letters; pastiness; emphasis in the middle or lower zones; irregularity; general signs of unreliability.

Thriftiness: narrow left margin; narrow spacing between words and lines; terminal strokes short or hooked.

Tolerance: garlands, small script; upright; short 't'-bars.

Traditionalism: left tendencies; ornamentation, pastiness; wide margins; slowness; regularity.

Trust: right slant; right tendencies; garlands; rising lines; highly-placed 'i'-dots and 't'-bars; wide script; even heavy pressure; extended terminals.

Uncommittedness: upright script; thready connection; uneven pressure; ambiguous letter-formations; variable writing angle; variable zonal emphasis.

Unrestrained Communicativeness: negative interpretations of right tending movements in the middle zone; exaggerated terminal strokes; excessively connected script; wide script; rising lines; garlands or threads.

Unselfishness: right slant; simplification; smallness; regularity; garlands; sharpness or pastiness; firm even pressure; good distribution of spaces; modest formation of capital 'I'; also of initials.

Utopianism: negative interpretation of fullness in the upper zone; negative interpretation of disconnected script.

Versatility: originality; disconnected script; thready connection; mixed writing systems.

Vision: fullness in the upper zone; highly-placed 't'-bars and 'i'-dots; simplification; good distribution of spaces.

Vitality: sharpness; pressure with irregularity; narrow right margins; heavy pressure; wide script with pressure; straight or rising lines; speed.

Vivacity: speed; wide script with pressure; irregularity; pastiness; rising lines; high-placed and/or rising 'i'-dots and 't'-bars; ornamentation.

Vulgarity: artificiality; heavy pressure; ornamentation; very poor distribution of spaces; oversized capitals; oversized signature and initials; much underlining.

Warm Nature: fullness in the middle zone; pastiness; irregularity.

Weakness: negative interpretation of right tendencies in the middle zone; low pressure with irregularity.

Will Power: large size with regularity; heavy pressure with regularity; firm strokes; heavy 'i'-dots; heavy and extended 't'-bars; rising lines; positive interpretation of hooks.

Wit: absence of angles; curves; wavy strokes.

Yieldingness: negative interpretation of low pressure with regularity; positive interpretation of left slant; narrow script; regularity; simplification; small script; capital 'I' written in the form of small 'i'; first strokes of 'M' and 'W' smaller than other strokes; low-placed 't'-bars.

Zeal: ascending lines; oversized middle zone with reduced upper and lower zones; large size with irregularity.

29 Table of Characteristics

Positive	Negative
Accuracy	exactingness
activity	restlessness
adaptability	superficiality
adventurousness	wanderlust
aesthetic sense	sensuousness
aggressiveness	overpowering forcefulness
agility	lability
altruism	utopianism
ambition	megalomania
amiability	two-facedness
analytical-mindedness	destructive criticism
anger	viciousness
asceticism	masochism
assertiveness	bossiness
authority	tyranny
balance	dullness
benevolence	do-gooding
broad-mindedness	vulgarity
calmness	casualness
carefulness	nervousness
caution	suspicion
chattiness	verbosity
chivalry	calculatingness
clarity	ceremoniousness
colourfulness	bombast
confidence	slavishness
conscientiousness	coldness
constancy	scruples
coolness	cockiness
contemplativeness	egocentricity
criticism	destructiveness
curiosity	nosiness
determination	ruthlessness
devotion	fanaticism
dexterity	cunning
diplomacy	insincerity
discussion	argumentation
dreaminess	distraction

116

Positive	Negative
economy	meanness
elasticity	inconstancy
elation	mania
emotional control	rigidity
enduringness	restlessness
energy	hedonism
enjoyment	obsession
enterprise	poker-face
enthusiasm	perversion
eroticism	scruples
ethical behaviour	opportunism
ethical demands	hysteria
excitability	pharisaism
family pride	clannishness
farsightedness	nervous anticipation
fatigue	feebleness
femininity	masochism
firmness	hardness
flexibility	indefiniteness
formality	externality
frankness	indiscretion
friendliness	familiarity
generosity	squeamishness
gentleness	lavishness
hardness	pitilessness
heartiness	bonhomie
hesitancy	indecision
hospitality	matiness
humility	self-negation
humour	irresponsibility
idealism	unrealism
imagination	irreality
impartiality	indefiniteness
imperiousness	domineeringness
impressionability	suggestibility
inactivity	inertia
independence	isolation
individuality	anarchy
informality	inconsiderateness
initiative	brashness
intuitive thinking	inconsequential thinking
inventiveness	cleverness
jest	silliness
jollification	irresponsibility
joviality	bonhomie
joy	ecstasy

TABLE OF CHARACTERISTICS

Positive	*Negative*
judiciousness	cleverness
justification	plausibility
keenness	sharpness
kindness	sentimentality
languidness	apathy
largess	extravagance
lassitude	boredom
leniency	laxness
lethargy	laziness
liberty	licence
loftiness	impracticality
loquaciousness	verbosity
loyalty	fanaticism
lucidity	aridity
mannerism	formalism
masculinity	sadism
materiality	earthiness
maturity	resignation
methodicalness	pedantry
mimicry	flattery
moderateness	colourlessness
modesty	timidity
moodiness	lability
naturalness	rashness
neighbourliness	matiness
neutrality	indifference
normality	dullness
open-mindedness	indecision
optimism	unrealism
orderliness	obsessionalism
originality	crankiness
ornamentation	ostentation
passion	emotional extravagance
patience	scruples
perseverance	obstinacy
pessimism	depression
poise	artificiality
possessiveness	jealousy
precaution	withdrawal
pride	pomp
progressiveness	radicalism
prudence	fear
quaintness	singularity
querulousness	quarrelsomeness

118

Positive	Negative
radicalism	anarchism
rationality	coldness, lack of imagination
realism	pessimism
receptivity	impressionability
reproductive intelligence	lack of initiative
reserve	distrust
resistance	awkwardness
resoluteness	defiance
respectfulness	compliance
restraint	inhibition
routine	automatism
secretiveness	suspiciousness
self-discipline	masochism
sensitiveness	crudeness
sensuality	addiction
sensuousness	weakness
seriousness	heaviness
shyness	hypersensitivity
simplicity	neglect
sincerity	tactlessness
sociability	matiness
spirituality	religiosity
steadiness	inertia
submissiveness	passivity
superiority	arrogance
sympathy	subjectivity
tactfulness	duplicity
taste	affectation
tenacity	obstinacy
thoughtfulness	theoreticality
thriftiness	meanness
tolerance	indifference
traditionalism	rigidity
trust	neglect
uncommittedness	indifference
unrestrained communicativeness	verbosity
unselfishness	self-negation
utopianism	unrealism
versatility	unsteadiness
vision	dreaminess
vitality	excitability
vivacity	instability
warm nature	amiability
wit	silliness
yieldingness	compliance
zeal	fanaticism

30 Bibliography

Albertini, L.: LEHRBUCH DER GRAPHOLOGIE, Stuttgart, 1932.

Allport, G. W.: PERSONALITY—A PSYCHOLOGICAL INTERPRETATION, New York, 1937.

Allport, G. W. & Vernon, P. E.: STUDIES IN EXPRESSIVE MOVEMENT, New York, 1933.

Bagger, E. S.: PSYCHO-GRAPHOLOGY: A STUDY OF RAFAEL ESCHERMANN, London, 1924.

Baldi, C.: TRATTADO COME DA UNA LETTERA MISSIVA SI CONOSCANO LA NATURA E QUALITA DELLO SCRIVIENTE, Bologna, 1644.

Barratinskaya, M. S.: CHARACTER AS REVEALED BY HANDWRITING, London, 1924.

Baughan, R.: CHARACTER INDICATED BY HANDWRITING, London, 1890.

Becker, M.: GRAPHOLOGIE DER KINDERHANDSCHRIFT, Freiburg, 1926.

Beroud, G.: L'EXPERTISE DES FAUX EN ECRITURE PAR ALTERATION, Lyon, 1923.

Berri, M de: THE SECRETS OF THE ALPHABET: A STUDY IN GRAPHOLOGY, New York, 1942.

Binet, A. L.: LES REVELATIONS DE L'ECRITURE D'APRES UN CONTROLE SCIENTIFIQUE, Paris, 1906.

Bobertag, C.: IST DIE GRAPHOLOGIE ZUVERLAESSIG? Heidelberg, 1929.

Booth, G. C.: HOW TO READ CHARACTER IN HANDWRITING, Philadelphia, 1910.

Brooks, C. H.: YOUR CHARACTER FROM YOUR HANDWRITING, London, 1946.

Bunker, M. N.: CASE BOOK NUMBER ONE, American Institute of Grapho-Analysis, Kansas City, 1936.

Byerly, T.: CHARACTERISTIC SIGNATURES, London, 1823.

Byram, J. H.: CHARACTER, New Jersey, 1935.

Callewaert, H.: PHYSIOLOGIE DE L'ECRITURE CURSIVE, Bruxelles, 1937.

Bürger, M: DIE HAND DES KRANKEN (pages 79-86), Munich, 1956.

Carvalho, C.: CRIME IN INK, New York, 1929.

Caspar, P. & Kügelgen, G. v: DICHTER IN DER HANDSCHRIFT, Hannover, 1937.

Crepieux-Jamin, J.: L'ECRITURE ET LE CRACTERE, Paris, 1888.
  HANDWRITING AND EXPRESSION, London, 1892.
  LES ELEMENTS DE L'ECRITURE DES CANAILLES, Paris, 1924.
  L'AGE ET LE SEX DANS L'ECRITURE, Paris, 1925.
  THE PSYCHOLOGY OF THE MOVEMENTS OF HANDWRITING, London, 1926.
  ABC DE LA GRAPHOLOGIE, Paris, 1930.

Davenport, B. F.: LOGICAL ANALYSIS OF SUBSCRIBED SIGNATURES, Boston, 1914.

Desbarolles, A.: SYSTEME DE GRAPHOLOGIE, Paris, 1875.
  METHODE PRACTIQUE DE GRAPHOLOGIE, Paris, 1878.

De Witt, B. L.: HANDWRITING AND CHARACTER, Philadelphia, 1925.

Donnini, R.: IL CARATTERE RIVELATO DELLA SCRITTURA, Perugia, 1925.

Douglas, A. W.: WHAT'S IN A SIGNATURE? Saint Louis, 1931.

Downey, J.: GRAPHOLOGY AND THE PSYCHOLOGY OF HANDWRITING, Baltimore, 1919.

Duparchy Jeannez, M.: L'EXPRESSION DE MALADIE DANS L'ECRITURE, Paris, 1919.

Duraud, M.: DE L'ECRITURE EN MIROIR, ETUDE SURL'ECRITURE DE LA MAIN GAUCHE DANS SES RAPPORTS AVEC L'APHASIE, 1882.

Eaton, S.: HOW TO READ CHARACTER FROM HANDWRITING, Boston, 1893.

Eng., H.: THE PSYCHOLOGY OF CHILDREN'S DRAWINGS, New York, 1931.

Erlenmeyer, D.: DIE SCHRIFT: GRUNDZUEGE IHRER PHYSIOLOGIE UND PATHOLOGIE, Stuttgart, 1879.

Erskine, L. G.: YOUR SIGNATURE: WHAT IT REVEALS, Larchmont, 1931.

Fischer, O.: EXPERIMENTE MIT RAPHAEL SCHERMANN, Vienna, 1924.

Frazer, P.: A MANUAL OF THE STUDY OF DOCUMENTS TO ESTABLISH THE INDIVIDUAL CHARACTER OF HANDWRITING AND TO DETECT FRAUD AND FORGERY, Philadelphia, 1894.

French, W. L.: THE PSYCHOLOGY OF HANDWRITING, London, 1922.

Frith, H.: HOW TO READ CHARACTER IN HANDWRITING, London, 1889

Furman, M. & Priv, Z. N.: HANDWRITING AND CHARACTER, London, 1930.

Fursac, J. R. de: LES ECRITS ET LES DESSINS DANS LES MALADIES NERVEUSES ET MENTALES, Paris, 1905.

Gerstner, H.: LEHRBUCH DER GRAPHOLOGIE, Celle, 1925.

Giraud, A.: PETIT DICTIONNAIRE DE GRAPHOLOGIE, Paris, 1896.

Hagen, H. von: READING CHARACTER FROM HANDWRITING, New York, 1902.

Hegar, W.: GRAPHOLOGIE PAR LE TRAIT, Paris, 1938.

Heider, J.: EXAKTE GRAPHOLOGIE, Bern-Leipzig, 1941.

Heiss, R.: DIE DEUTUNG DER HANDSCHRIFT, Hamburg, 1943.

Hocquart, E.: L'ART DE JUGER DE L'ESPRIT ET DU CARACTERE DES HOMMES SUR LEUR ECRITURE, Paris, 1812.

Hughes, A. E.: SELF-ANALYSIS FROM YOUR HANDWRITING, London, 1966.

Jacoby, H. J.: HANDSCHRIFT UND SEXUALITAET, Berlin, 1932.

ANALYSIS OF HANDWRITING: AN INTRODUCTION INTO SCIENTIFIC GRAPHOLOGY, London, 1939.

SELF-KNOWLEDGE THROUGH HANDWRITING, New York, 1941.

Karfeld, K. P.: DAS WUNDER DER HANDSCHRIFT, Berlin, 1935.

Klages, L.: DIE PROBLEME DER GRAPHOLOGIE, Leipzig, 1910.

AUSDRUCKSBEWEGUNG UND GESTALTUNGSKRAFT, Leipzig, 1913.

EINFUEHRUNG IN DIE PSYCHOLOGIE DER HANDSCHRIFT, Heilbronn, 1924.

DIE GRUNDLAGEN DER CHARAKTERKUNDE, Leipzig, 1928.

HANDSCHRIFT UND CHARAKTER: GEMEINVERSTAENDLICHER ABRISS DER GRAPHOLOGISCHEN TECHNIK, Leipzig, 1940.

Koch, U.: TRATTATO SCIENTIFICO DE GRAFOLOGIA, Bologna, 1920.

Korff, E.: HANDSCHRIFTKUNDE UND CHARAKTERERKENNTNIS, Bad Homburg, 1936.

Koster, R.: DIE SCHRIFT BEI GEISTESKRANKHEITEN, Leipzig, 1903.

Langenbruch, M.: PRAKTISCHE MENSCHENKENNTNIS AUF GRUND DER HANDSCHRIFT, Berlin, 1929.

Lavater, J. K.: PHYSIOGNOMISCHE FRAGMENTE, Leipzig, 1774-78.

Lavay, J. B.: DISPUTED HANDWRITING, Chicago, 1909.

Leibl, M.: GRAFOLOGIA PSICOLOGICA, Milan, 1935.

Lewinson, T. S. & Zubin, J.: HANDWRITING ANALYSIS: A SERIES OF SCALES FOR EVALUATING THE DYNAMIC ASPECTS OF HANDWRITING, New York, 1942.

Lombroso, C.: GRAFOLOGIA, Milan, 1895.

HANDBUCH DER GRAPHOLOGIE, Leipzig, 1902.

Lumley, E.: THE ART OF JUDGING THE CHARACTER OF INDIVIDUALS FROM THEIR HANDWRITING AND STYLE, London, 1875.

Marcuse, L.: APPLIED GRAPHOLOGY, New York, 1945.

Margadant, S. V.: EINE TIEFENPSYCHOLOGISCHE GRUNDLAGE ZUR KLAGES'SCHEN

BIBLIOGRAPHY

GRAPHOLOGIE, Amsterdam, 1938.

Marguerite, R. & Mannheim, M. J.: VINCENT VAN GOCH IM SPIEGEL SEINER HANDSCHRIFT, Basel, 1938.

Mayer, G. & Schneickert, H.: DIE WISSENSCHAFTLICHEN GRUNDLAGEN DER GRAPHOLOGIE, Jena, 1940.

Mendel, A. O.: PERSONALITY IN HANDWRITING, New York, 1947.

Mendelsohn, A. & G.: DER MENSCH IN DER HANDSCHRIFT, Leipzig, 1928.

Meyer, G.: DIE WISSENSCHAFTLICHEN GRUNDLAGEN DER GRAPHOLOGIE: VOR-SCHULE DER GERICHTLICHEN SCHRIFTVERGLEICHUNG, Jena, 1940.

Meyer, J.: MIND YOUR P'S AND Q'S, New York, 1927.

Michon, J. H.: SYSTEME DE GRAPHOLOGIE, Paris, 1875.
LA METHODE PRACTIQUE DE GRAPHOLOGIE, Paris, 1878.

Morf, G.: PRAKTISCHE CHARAKTERKUNDE, Bern, 1945.

Müller, W. H. & Enskat, A.: GRAPHOLOGISCHE DIAGNOSTIK, Bern, 1961.

Myer, O. N.: THE LANGUAGE OF HANDWRITING, London, 1958.

Newell, H. A.: YOUR SIGNATURE: A GUIDE TO CHARACTER FROM HANDWRITING, London, 1926.

Noel M.: THE TRAIL YOU LEAVE IN INK, Kansas City, 1941-46.

Olyanowa, N.: HANDWRITING TELLS, New York, 1936.
THE PSYCHOLOGY OF HANDWRITING, New York, 1960.

Paisley, M. A.: PROBLEMS IN CURSIVE, MANUSCRIPT AND MIRROR WRITING, Winston-Salem, 1937.

Piscart, R.: ECHELLE OBJECTIVE D'ECRITURE, Louvain, 1939.

Pophal, R.: GRUNDLEGUNG DER BEWEGUNGSPHYSIOLOGISCHEN GRAPHOLOGIE, Leipzig, 1939.

Preyer, W. T.: ZUR PSYCHOLOGIE DES SCHREIBENS, Hamburg, 1895.

Proskauer, G.: GRAPHOMETRISCHE UNTERSUCHUNGEN BEI GESUNDEN, SCHIZO-PHRENEN UND MANISCH-DEPRESSIVEN, Berlin, 1936.

Pulver, M.: TRIEB UND VERBRECHEN IN DER HANDSCHRIFT, Zürich, 1934.
SYMBOLIK DER HANDSCHRIFT, Zürich, Leipzig, 1940.
INTELLIGENZ IM SCHRIFTAUSDRUCK, Zürich, 1949.

Rand, H. A.: GRAPHOLOGY, Cambridge, Mass., 1947.

Reis, H.: DIE HANDSCHRIFT—DEIN CHARAKTER, Bad Homburg, 1940.

Rexford, G.: WHAT HANDWRITING INDICATES, New York, 1904.

Rice, L.: CHARACTER READING FROM HANDWRITING, New York, 1904.

Roman, K. G.: HANDWRITING: A KEY TO PERSONALITY, London, 1954.

Rougemont, E. de: UNE NOUVELLE SCIENCE SOCIALE, LA GRAPHOLOGIE, COURS GRADUE PROFESSE AU COLLEGE LIBRE DES SCIENCES SOCIALES, Paris, 1932.

Sara, D.: HANDWRITING: A PERSONALITY GUIDE, London, 1969.

Saudek, R.: THE PSYCHOLOGY OF HANDWRITING, London, 1925-28.
EXPERIMENTS WITH HANDWRITING, London, 1928.

Schermann, R.: DIE SCHRIFT LUEGT NICHT, Berlin, 1929.
SCHICKSALE DES LEBENS, Berlin, 1932.

Schneidemühl, G.: HANDSCHRIFT UND CHARAKTER: EIN LEHRBUCH DER HAND-SCHRIFTENBEURTEILUNG, Leipzig, 1911.

Schneikert, H.: LEITFADEN DER GERICHTLICHEN SCHRIFTVERGLEICHUNG, Leipzig, 1918.

Schuler, R. A.: MUSSOLINI A TRAVERS SON ECRITURE, Paris, 1925.

Schultze-Naumburg, B.: HANDSCHRIFT UND EHE, Munich, 1932.

Seeling, O.: ZWILLINGSINDIVIDUALITAET UND ZWILLINGSGEMEINSCHAT, Hamburg, 1932.

Severino, M. A.: VATICINATOR, SIVE TRACTATUS DE DIVINATIONE LITTERALI, 17th century treatise on divination from letters.

Silver, A. H.: GRAPHOGRAMS FOR INSTANT ANALYSIS OF CHARACTER THROUGH HANDWRITING, London, 1928.

Singer, E.: THE GRAPHOLOGIST'S ALPHABET, London, 1950.

HANDWRITING AND MARRIAGE, London, 1953.

PERSONALITY IN HANDWRITING, London, 1954.

Smith, A. J.: APPLIED GRAPHOLOGY, Chicago, 1920.

Solange-Pellat, E.: LES LOIS DEL L'ECRITURE, Paris, 1927.

Sonnemann, U.: HANDWRITING ANALYSIS, New York, 1950.

Spencer, S.: WHAT HANDWRITING REVEALS, New York, 1927.

Stern, W.: PERSON UND SACHE, Leipzig, 1923.

Stocker, R. D.: THE LANGUAGE OF HANDWRITING, New York, 1901.

Storey, A.: A MANUAL OF GRAPHOLOGY, London, 1922.

Streletski, C.: GRAPHOLOGIE DU PRACTICIEN, Paris, 1927.

Strelisker, G.: DAS ERLEBNIS DER HANDSCHRIFT, Leipzig/Vienna/Berlin, 1934.

DIE DEUTBARKEIT DER SCHUELERHANDSCHRIFT, Hamburg, 1932.

KRANKHEITSMERKMALE IN DER HANDSCHRIFT, Hamburg, 1932.

SELBSTBESPIEGELUNG IN DER HANDSCHRIFT, Hamburg, 1932.

AUCH IN DER KRITZELEI LIEGT EIN TIEFERER SINN, Berlin, 1931.

Tchang, T. M.: L'ECRITURE CHINOISE ET LE GESTE HUMAIN: ESSAI SUR LA FORMATION DE L'ECRITURE CHINOISE, Shanghai, 1937.

Teillard, A.: L'AME ET L'ECRITURE, Paris, 1948.

HANDSCHRIFTENDEUTUNG AUF TIEFENPSYCHOLOGISCHER GRUNDLAGE, Munich, 1952.

Teltscher, H. O.: HANDWRITING: THE KEY TO SUCCESSFUL LIVING, New York, 1942.

Thumm-Kintzel, M.: PSYCHOLOGY AND PATHOLOGY OF HANDWRITING, New York, 1905.

Trey, M. de: DER WILLE IN DER HANDSCHRIFT, Bern, 1946.

Ungern-Sternberg, I. C.: PORTRAIT INTIME D'UN ECRIVAIN D'APRES SIX LIGNES DE SON ECRITURE, Paris, 1898.

Vanzanges, L. M.: L'ECRITURE DES MUSICIANS CELEBRES, Paris, 1913.

L'ECRITURE DES CREATEURS INTELLECTUELS, Paris, 1926.

Vertesi, E.: HANDSCHRIFT UND EIGENART DER KREBSGEFAETRDETEN, Budapest, 1939.

Victor, F.: HANDWRITING: A PERSONALITY PROJECTION, Springfield, 1952.

Wieser, R.: DER RHYTHMUS IN DER VERBRECHERHANDSCHRIFT SYSTEMATISCH DARGESTELLT AN 694 SCHRIFTEN KRIMINELLER UND 200 SCHRIFTEN KRIMINELLER UND 200 SCHRIFTEN NICHT-KRIMINILLER, Leipzig, 1938.

Wittlich, B.: HANDSCHRIFT UND ERZIEHUNG, Berlin/Leipzig, 1940.

ANGEWANDTE GRAPHOLOGIE, Berlin West, 1951.

Wolff, W.: THE EXPRESSION OF PERSONALITY: EXPERIMENTAL DEPTH PSYCHOLOGY, New York, 1943.

DIAGRAMS OF THE UNCONSCIOUS, New York, 1948.

Wormser, P.: DIE BEURTEILUNG DER HANDSCHRIFT IN DER PSYCHIATRIE, Zürich, 1947.

A PERSONAL WORD FROM MELVIN POWERS
PUBLISHER, WILSHIRE BOOK COMPANY

Dear Friend:

My goal is to publish interesting, informative, and in-spirational books. You can help me accomplish this by answering the following questions, either by phone or by mail. Or, if convenient for you, I would welcome the oppor-tunity to visit with you in my office and hear your com-ments in person.

Did you enjoy reading this book? Why?

Would you enjoy reading another similar book?

What idea in the book impressed you the most?

If applicable to your situation, have you incorporated this idea in your daily life?

Is there a chapter that could serve as a theme for an entire book? Please explain.

If you have an idea for a book, I would welcome dis-cussing it with you. If you already have one in progress, write or call me concerning possible publication. I can be reached at (213) 875-1711 or (213) 983-1105.

Sincerely yours,

MELVIN POWERS

12015 Sherman Road
North Hollywood, California 91605

MELVIN POWERS SELF-IMPROVEMENT LIBRARY

ASTROLOGY
____ASTROLOGY: HOW TO CHART YOUR HOROSCOPE *Max Heindel*   3.00
____ASTROLOGY: YOUR PERSONAL SUN-SIGN GUIDE *Beatrice Ryder*   3.00
____ASTROLOGY FOR EVERYDAY LIVING *Janet Harris*   2.00
____ASTROLOGY MADE EASY *Astarte*   3.00
____ASTROLOGY MADE PRACTICAL *Alexandra Kayhle*   3.00
____ASTROLOGY, ROMANCE, YOU AND THE STARS *Anthony Norvell*   4.00
____MY WORLD OF ASTROLOGY *Sydney Omarr*   5.00
____THOUGHT DIAL *Sydney Omarr*   4.00
____WHAT THE STARS REVEAL ABOUT THE MEN IN YOUR LIFE *Thelma White*   3.00

BRIDGE
____BRIDGE BIDDING MADE EASY *Edwin B. Kantar*   7.00
____BRIDGE CONVENTIONS *Edwin B. Kantar*   5.00
____BRIDGE HUMOR *Edwin B. Kantar*   5.00
____COMPETITIVE BIDDING IN MODERN BRIDGE *Edgar Kaplan*   4.00
____DEFENSIVE BRIDGE PLAY COMPLETE *Edwin B. Kantar*   10.00
____GAMESMAN BRIDGE—Play Better with Kantar *Edwin B. Kantar*   5.00
____HOW TO IMPROVE YOUR BRIDGE *Alfred Sheinwold*   3.00
____IMPROVING YOUR BIDDING SKILLS *Edwin B. Kantar*   4.00
____INTRODUCTION TO DEFENDER'S PLAY *Edwin B. Kantar*   3.00
____SHORT CUT TO WINNING BRIDGE *Alfred Sheinwold*   3.00
____TEST YOUR BRIDGE PLAY *Edwin B. Kantar*   5.00
____VOLUME 2—TEST YOUR BRIDGE PLAY *Edwin B. Kantar*   5.00
____WINNING DECLARER PLAY *Dorothy Hayden Truscott*   4.00

BUSINESS, STUDY & REFERENCE
____CONVERSATION MADE EASY *Elliot Russell*   3.00
____EXAM SECRET *Dennis B. Jackson*   3.00
____FIX-IT BOOK *Arthur Symons*   2.00
____HOW TO DEVELOP A BETTER SPEAKING VOICE *M. Hellier*   3.00
____HOW TO MAKE A FORTUNE IN REAL ESTATE *Albert Winnikoff*   4.00
____INCREASE YOUR LEARNING POWER *Geoffrey A. Dudley*   3.00
____MAGIC OF NUMBERS *Robert Tocquet*   2.00
____PRACTICAL GUIDE TO BETTER CONCENTRATION *Melvin Powers*   3.00
____PRACTICAL GUIDE TO PUBLIC SPEAKING *Maurice Forley*   3.00
____7 DAYS TO FASTER READING *William S. Schaill*   3.00
____SONGWRITERS RHYMING DICTIONARY *Jane Shaw Whitfield*   5.00
____SPELLING MADE EASY *Lester D. Basch & Dr. Milton Finkelstein*   2.00
____STUDENT'S GUIDE TO BETTER GRADES *J. A. Rickard*   3.00
____TEST YOURSELF—Find Your Hidden Talent *Jack Shafer*   3.00
____YOUR WILL & WHAT TO DO ABOUT IT *Attorney Samuel G. Kling*   3.00

CALLIGRAPHY
____ADVANCED CALLIGRAPHY *Katherine Jeffares*   7.00
____CALLIGRAPHER'S REFERENCE BOOK *Anne Leptich & Jacque Evans*   7.00
____CALLIGRAPHY—The Art of Beautiful Writing *Katherine Jeffares*   7.00
____CALLIGRAPHY FOR FUN & PROFIT *Anne Leptich & Jacque Evans*   7.00
____CALLIGRAPHY MADE EASY *Tina Serafini*   7.00

CHESS & CHECKERS
____BEGINNER'S GUIDE TO WINNING CHESS *Fred Reinfeld*   3.00
____CHECKERS MADE EASY *Tom Wiswell*   2.00
____CHESS IN TEN EASY LESSONS *Larry Evans*   3.00
____CHESS MADE EASY *Milton L. Hanauer*   3.00
____CHESS PROBLEMS FOR BEGINNERS *edited by Fred Reinfeld*   2.00
____CHESS SECRETS REVEALED *Fred Reinfeld*   2.00
____CHESS STRATEGY—An Expert's Guide *Fred Reinfeld*   2.00
____CHESS TACTICS FOR BEGINNERS *edited by Fred Reinfeld*   3.00
____CHESS THEORY & PRACTICE *Morry & Mitchell*   2.00
____HOW TO WIN AT CHECKERS *Fred Reinfeld*   3.00
____1001 BRILLIANT WAYS TO CHECKMATE *Fred Reinfeld*   4.00
____1001 WINNING CHESS SACRIFICES & COMBINATIONS *Fred Reinfeld*   4.00
____SOVIET CHESS *Edited by R. G. Wade*   3.00

COOKERY & HERBS

____CULPEPER'S HERBAL REMEDIES *Dr. Nicholas Culpeper*   3.00
____FAST GOURMET COOKBOOK *Poppy Cannon*   2.50
____GINSENG The Myth & The Truth *Joseph P. Hou*   3.00
____HEALING POWER OF HERBS *May Bethel*   3.00
____HEALING POWER OF NATURAL FOODS *May Bethel*   3.00
____HERB HANDBOOK *Dawn MacLeod*   3.00
____HERBS FOR COOKING AND HEALING *Dr. Donald Law*   2.00
____HERBS FOR HEALTH—How to Grow & Use Them *Louise Evans Doole*   3.00
____HOME GARDEN COOKBOOK—Delicious Natural Food Recipes *Ken Kraft*   3.00
____MEDICAL HERBALIST *edited by Dr. J. R. Yemm*   3.00
____NATURAL FOOD COOKBOOK *Dr. Harry C. Bond*   3.00
____NATURE'S MEDICINES *Richard Lucas*   3.00
____VEGETABLE GARDENING FOR BEGINNERS *Hugh Wiberg*   2.00
____VEGETABLES FOR TODAY'S GARDENS *R. Milton Carleton*   2.00
____VEGETARIAN COOKERY *Janet Walker*   4.00
____VEGETARIAN COOKING MADE EASY & DELECTABLE *Veronica Vezza*   3.00
____VEGETARIAN DELIGHTS—A Happy Cookbook for Health *K. R. Mehta*   2.00
____VEGETARIAN GOURMET COOKBOOK *Joyce McKinnel*   3.00

GAMBLING & POKER

____ADVANCED POKER STRATEGY & WINNING PLAY *A. D. Livingston*   5.00
____HOW NOT TO LOSE AT POKER *Jeffrey Lloyd Castle*   3.00
____HOW TO WIN AT DICE GAMES *Skip Frey*   3.00
____HOW TO WIN AT POKER *Terence Reese & Anthony T. Watkins*   3.00
____SECRETS OF WINNING POKER *George S. Coffin*   3.00
____WINNING AT CRAPS *Dr. Lloyd T. Commins*   3.00
____WINNING AT GIN *Chester Wander & Cy Rice*   3.00
____WINNING AT POKER—An Expert's Guide *John Archer*   3.00
____WINNING AT 21—An Expert's Guide *John Archer*   5.00
____WINNING POKER SYSTEMS *Norman Zadeh*   3.00

HEALTH

____BEE POLLEN *Lynda Lyngheim & Jack Scagnetti*   3.00
____DR. LINDNER'S SPECIAL WEIGHT CONTROL METHOD *P. G. Lindner, M.D.*   1.50
____HELP YOURSELF TO BETTER SIGHT *Margaret Darst Corbett*   3.00
____HOW TO IMPROVE YOUR VISION *Dr. Robert A. Kraskin*   3.00
____HOW YOU CAN STOP SMOKING PERMANENTLY *Ernest Caldwell*   3.00
____MIND OVER PLATTER *Peter G. Lindner, M.D.*   3.00
____NATURE'S WAY TO NUTRITION & VIBRANT HEALTH *Robert J. Scrutton*   3.00
____NEW CARBOHYDRATE DIET COUNTER *Patti Lopez-Pereira*   1.50
____QUICK & EASY EXERCISES FOR FACIAL BEAUTY *Judy Smith-deal*   2.00
____QUICK & EASY EXERCISES FOR FIGURE BEAUTY *Judy Smith-deal*   2.00
____REFLEXOLOGY *Dr. Maybelle Segal*   3.00
____REFLEXOLOGY FOR GOOD HEALTH *Anna Kaye & Don C. Matchan*   3.00
____YOU CAN LEARN TO RELAX *Dr. Samuel Gutwirth*   3.00
____YOUR ALLERGY—What To Do About It *Allan Knight, M.D.*   3.00

HOBBIES

____BEACHCOMBING FOR BEGINNERS *Norman Hickin*   2.00
____BLACKSTONE'S MODERN CARD TRICKS *Harry Blackstone*   3.00
____BLACKSTONE'S SECRETS OF MAGIC *Harry Blackstone*   3.00
____COIN COLLECTING FOR BEGINNERS *Burton Hobson & Fred Reinfeld*   3.00
____ENTERTAINING WITH ESP *Tony 'Doc' Shiels*   2.00
____400 FASCINATING MAGIC TRICKS YOU CAN DO *Howard Thurston*   3.00
____HOW I TURN JUNK INTO FUN AND PROFIT *Sari*   3.00
____HOW TO WRITE A HIT SONG & SELL IT *Tommy Boyce*   7.00
____JUGGLING MADE EASY *Rudolf Dittrich*   2.00
____MAGIC FOR ALL AGES *Walter Gibson*   4.00
____MAGIC MADE EASY *Byron Wels*   2.00
____STAMP COLLECTING FOR BEGINNERS *Burton Hobson*   2.00

HORSE PLAYERS' WINNING GUIDES

____BETTING HORSES TO WIN *Les Conklin*   3.00
____ELIMINATE THE LOSERS *Bob McKnight*   3.00
____HOW TO PICK WINNING HORSES *Bob McKnight*   3.00

_____HOW TO RAISE AN EMOTIONALLY HEALTHY, HAPPY CHILD *A. Ellis* 4.00
_____SEX WITHOUT GUILT *Albert Ellis, Ph.D.* 5.00
_____SEXUALLY ADEQUATE MALE *Frank S. Caprio, M.D.* 3.00

MELVIN POWERS' MAIL ORDER LIBRARY

_____HOW TO GET RICH IN MAIL ORDER *Melvin Powers* 10.00
_____HOW TO WRITE A GOOD ADVERTISEMENT *Victor O. Schwab* 15.00
_____MAIL ORDER MADE EASY *J. Frank Brumbaugh* 10.00
_____U.S. MAIL ORDER SHOPPER'S GUIDE *Susan Spitzer* 10.00

METAPHYSICS & OCCULT

_____BOOK OF TALISMANS, AMULETS & ZODIACAL GEMS *William Pavitt* 5.00
_____CONCENTRATION—A Guide to Mental Mastery *Mouni Sadhu* 4.00
_____CRITIQUES OF GOD *Edited by Peter Angeles* 7.00
_____DREAMS & OMENS REVEALED *Fred Gettings* 3.00
_____EXTRA-TERRESTRIAL INTELLIGENCE—The First Encounter 6.00
_____FORTUNE TELLING WITH CARDS *P. Foli* 3.00
_____HANDWRITING ANALYSIS MADE EASY *John Marley* 3.00
_____HANDWRITING TELLS *Nadya Olyanova* 5.00
_____HOW TO UNDERSTAND YOUR DREAMS *Geoffrey A. Dudley* 3.00
_____ILLUSTRATED YOGA *William Zorn* 3.00
_____IN DAYS OF GREAT PEACE *Mouni Sadhu* 3.00
_____KING SOLOMON'S TEMPLE IN THE MASONIC TRADITION *Alex Horne* 5.00
_____LSD—THE AGE OF MIND *Bernard Roseman* 2.00
_____MAGICIAN—His training and work *W. E. Butler* 3.00
_____MEDITATION *Mouni Sadhu* 5.00
_____MODERN NUMEROLOGY *Morris C. Goodman* 3.00
_____NUMEROLOGY—ITS FACTS AND SECRETS *Ariel Yvon Taylor* 3.00
_____NUMEROLOGY MADE EASY *W. Mykian* 3.00
_____PALMISTRY MADE EASY *Fred Gettings* 3.00
_____PALMISTRY MADE PRACTICAL *Elizabeth Daniels Squire* 4.00
_____PALMISTRY SECRETS REVEALED *Henry Frith* 3.00
_____PROPHECY IN OUR TIME *Martin Ebon* 2.50
_____PSYCHOLOGY OF HANDWRITING *Nadya Olyanova* 5.00
_____SUPERSTITION—Are you superstitious? *Eric Maple* 2.00
_____TAROT *Mouni Sadhu* 6.00
_____TAROT OF THE BOHEMIANS *Papus* 5.00
_____WAYS TO SELF-REALIZATION *Mouni Sadhu* 3.00
_____WHAT YOUR HANDWRITING REVEALS *Albert E. Hughes* 3.00
_____WITCHCRAFT, MAGIC & OCCULTISM—A Fascinating History *W. B. Crow* 5.00
_____WITCHCRAFT—THE SIXTH SENSE *Justine Glass* 4.00
_____WORLD OF PSYCHIC RESEARCH *Hereward Carrington* 2.00

SELF-HELP & INSPIRATIONAL

_____DAILY POWER FOR JOYFUL LIVING *Dr. Donald Curtis* 3.00
_____DYNAMIC THINKING *Melvin Powers* 2.00
_____EXUBERANCE—Your Guide to Happiness & Fulfillment *Dr. Paul Kurtz* 3.00
_____GREATEST POWER IN THE UNIVERSE *U. S. Andersen* 5.00
_____GROW RICH WHILE YOU SLEEP *Ben Sweetland* 3.00
_____GROWTH THROUGH REASON. *Albert Ellis, Ph.D.* 4.00
_____GUIDE TO DEVELOPING YOUR POTENTIAL *Herbert A. Otto, Ph.D.* 3.00
_____GUIDE TO LIVING IN BALANCE *Frank S. Caprio, M.D.* 2.00
_____HELPING YOURSELF WITH APPLIED PSYCHOLOGY *R. Henderson* 2.00
_____HELPING YOURSELF WITH PSYCHIATRY *Frank S. Caprio, M.D.* 2.00
_____HOW TO ATTRACT GOOD LUCK *A. H. Z. Carr* 4.00
_____HOW TO CONTROL YOUR DESTINY *Norvell* 3.00
_____HOW TO DEVELOP A WINNING PERSONALITY *Martin Panzer* 3.00
_____HOW TO DEVELOP AN EXCEPTIONAL MEMORY *Young & Gibson* 4.00
_____HOW TO OVERCOME YOUR FEARS *M. P. Leahy, M.D.* 3.00
_____HOW YOU CAN HAVE CONFIDENCE AND POWER *Les Giblin* 3.00
_____HUMAN PROBLEMS & HOW TO SOLVE THEM *Dr. Donald Curtis* 4.00
_____I CAN *Ben Sweetland* 5.00
_____I WILL *Ben Sweetland* 3.00
_____LEFT-HANDED PEOPLE *Michael Barsley* 4.00
_____MAGIC IN YOUR MIND *U. S. Andersen* 5.00

____MAGIC OF THINKING BIG *Dr. David J. Schwartz*	3.00
____MAGIC POWER OF YOUR MIND *Walter M. Germain*	4.00
____MENTAL POWER THROUGH SLEEP SUGGESTION *Melvin Powers*	3.00
____NEW GUIDE TO RATIONAL LIVING *Albert Ellis, Ph.D. & R. Harper, Ph.D.*	3.00
____OUR TROUBLED SELVES *Dr. Allan Fromme*	3.00
____PSYCHO-CYBERNETICS *Maxwell Maltz, M.D.*	3.00
____SCIENCE OF MIND IN DAILY LIVING *Dr. Donald Curtis*	5.00
____SECRET OF SECRETS *U. S. Andersen*	5.00
____SECRET POWER OF THE PYRAMIDS *U. S. Andersen*	5.00
____STUTTERING AND WHAT YOU CAN DO ABOUT IT *W. Johnson, Ph.D.*	2.50
____SUCCESS-CYBERNETICS *U. S. Andersen*	4.00
____10 DAYS TO A GREAT NEW LIFE *William E. Edwards*	3.00
____THINK AND GROW RICH *Napoleon Hill*	3.00
____THREE MAGIC WORDS *U. S. Andersen*	5.00
____TREASURY OF COMFORT *edited by Rabbi Sidney Greenberg*	5.00
____TREASURY OF THE ART OF LIVING *Sidney S. Greenberg*	5.00
____YOU ARE NOT THE TARGET *Laura Huxley*	4.00
____YOUR SUBCONSCIOUS POWER *Charles M. Simmons*	5.00
____YOUR THOUGHTS CAN CHANGE YOUR LIFE *Dr. Donald Curtis*	4.00

SPORTS

____BICYCLING FOR FUN AND GOOD HEALTH *Kenneth E. Luther*	2.00
____BILLIARDS—Pocket • Carom • Three Cushion *Clive Cottingham, Jr.*	3.00
____CAMPING-OUT 101 Ideas & Activities *Bruno Knobel*	2.00
____COMPLETE GUIDE TO FISHING *Vlad Evanoff*	2.00
____HOW TO IMPROVE YOUR RACQUETBALL *Lubarsky, Kaufman, & Scagnetti*	3.00
____HOW TO WIN AT POCKET BILLIARDS *Edward D. Knuchell*	4.00
____JOY OF WALKING *Jack Scagnetti*	3.00
____LEARNING & TEACHING SOCCER SKILLS *Eric Worthington*	3.00
____MOTORCYCLING FOR BEGINNERS *I. G. Edmonds*	3.00
____RACQUETBALL FOR WOMEN *Toni Hudson, Jack Scagnetti & Vince Rondone*	3.00
____RACQUETBALL MADE EASY *Steve Lubarsky, Rod Delson & Jack Scagnetti*	3.00
____SECRET OF BOWLING STRIKES *Dawson Taylor*	3.00
____SECRET OF PERFECT PUTTING *Horton Smith & Dawson Taylor*	3.00
____SOCCER—The game & how to play it *Gary Rosenthal*	3.00
____STARTING SOCCER *Edward F. Dolan, Jr.*	3.00
____TABLE TENNIS MADE EASY *Johnny Leach*	2.00

TENNIS LOVERS' LIBRARY

____BEGINNER'S GUIDE TO WINNING TENNIS *Helen Hull Jacobs*	2.00
____HOW TO BEAT BETTER TENNIS PLAYERS *Loring Fiske*	4.00
____HOW TO IMPROVE YOUR TENNIS—Style, Strategy & Analysis *C. Wilson*	2.00
____INSIDE TENNIS—Techniques of Winning *Jim Leighton*	3.00
____PLAY TENNIS WITH ROSEWALL *Ken Rosewall*	2.00
____PSYCH YOURSELF TO BETTER TENNIS *Dr. Walter A. Luszki*	2.00
____SUCCESSFUL TENNIS *Neale Fraser*	2.00
____TENNIS FOR BEGINNERS *Dr. H. A. Murray*	2.00
____TENNIS MADE EASY *Joel Brecheen*	2.00
____WEEKEND TENNIS—How to have fun & win at the same time *Bill Talbert*	3.00
____WINNING WITH PERCENTAGE TENNIS—Smart Strategy *Jack Lowe*	2.00

WILSHIRE PET LIBRARY

____DOG OBEDIENCE TRAINING *Gust Kessopulos*	4.00
____DOG TRAINING MADE EASY & FUN *John W. Kellogg*	4.00
____HOW TO BRING UP YOUR PET DOG *Kurt Unkelbach*	2.00
____HOW TO RAISE & TRAIN YOUR PUPPY *Jeff Griffen*	2.00
____PIGEONS: HOW TO RAISE & TRAIN THEM *William H. Allen, Jr.*	2.00

*The books listed above can be obtained from your book dealer or directly from
Melvin Powers. When ordering, please remit 50¢ per book postage & handling.
Send for our free illustrated catalog of self-improvement books.*

Melvin Powers
12015 Sherman Road, No. Hollywood, California 91605

WILSHIRE HORSE LOVERS' LIBRARY

*The books listed above can be obtained from your book dealer or directly from
Melvin Powers. When ordering, please remit 50¢ per book postage & handling.
Send for our free illustrated catalog of self-improvement books.*

Melvin Powers
12015 Sherman Road, No. Hollywood, California 91605

NOTES

NOTES